I0760097

BABY FOOD BIBLE

FOR FRANKIE AND GEORGE,
OUR INSPIRATION FOR WRITING THIS BOOK.

BABY FOOD BIBLE

A NOURISHING GUIDE TO
FEEDING YOUR FAMILY, FROM FIRST BITE AND BEYOND

By Julia Tellidis and Lauren Skora of *Bable*

Hardie Grant
BOOKS

07 INTRODUCTION

08 A SOLID START

10 SETTING UP SOLID FOUNDATIONS
17 SPOON-FEEDING
20 BABY-LED WEANING
24 COMBO-FEEDING
26 GAGGING VS. CHOKING
28 HOW MUCH AND HOW OFTEN?
31 BREASTMILK, FORMULA AND OTHER LIQUIDS
32 PROCESSED BABY FOODS
35 MAKING SENSE OF SODIUM
36 MAKING SENSE OF SUGAR
38 SEASONING

40 FOOD ALLERGENS

42 HOW TO INTRODUCE THE TOP 9 ALLERGENS
45 HOW TO SPOT AN ALLERGIC REACTION
46 ALLERGEN MASTER GUIDE
50 ALLERGEN SWAPS

52 NOURISHING YOUR LITTLE ONE

54 ESSENTIAL NUTRIENTS
66 A BALANCED PLATE
72 FLOURISHING LITTLE GUTS
74 FOOD QUALITY
80 COMPARING FARMING PRACTICES
84 TOP TIPS FOR RAISING INTUITIVE EATERS

86 RECIPES

89 NOTES
90 KEY

92 BREAKFAST
130 PRAM PLEASERS
176 LUNCHBOXES
186 SMALL BITES
204 MAINS
248 SIDES AND CONDIMENTS
280 SWEETS

310 INDEX
316 THANKS
317 ABOUT THE AUTHORS

INTRODUCTION

Our story began on Bronte Beach in Sydney, Australia, just a few weeks before the arrival of our first babies. There we were, two heavily pregnant women hanging out with our friends, when we noticed each other across the sand. Three months later, with our newborns strapped to our chests, we recognised each other again in line at our local coffee shop. Little did we know that this second chance encounter would not only mark the beginning of our friendship, but also the start of our business, Bable (aka Baby Food Bible).

From that moment on, our lives became intertwined as we navigated motherhood together. Our babies were born just 3 weeks apart and we became each other's unwavering support system. Those first 6 months passed in survival mode as we tackled the challenges of newborn life. We focused on recovering from childbirth, learning the intricacies of breastfeeding and working out how to help our little ones thrive, all the while navigating the world of no sleep.

As we emerged from the trenches, we found ourselves grappling with a new challenge – starting solids. Lauren had a design background so when it came time to start her daughter, Frankie, on solids she wanted a better understanding of which vital nutrients her child needed to thrive. Inspired by her own research, she decided to study baby nutrition. Meanwhile, Jules was a clinical nutritionist but felt that her knowledge of 'food is medicine' was overwhelming when starting solids with her son, George.

We had countless conversations about the conflicting advice around starting solids and did lots of research between us, determined to get it right from the beginning. What was the best nutritional option when introducing solids? Purées or finger foods? Would the foods we introduced impact our children's future taste preferences? We quickly realised we were not alone and that lots of other parents also found the journey tricky.

Together we developed our own recipes, which were not only balanced and nutrient-dense, but also designed to please even the pickiest of eaters, as well as cater to the whole family. We started sharing our recipes and learnings online with friends who, like us, were searching for guidance. The response was overwhelming. It was clear that a resource providing simple delicious recipes and clear advice for starting solids was sorely needed.

We had found our purpose. With our shared passion for food and our desire to simplify the journey of starting solids and feeding the whole family, we knew we had to grow beyond our online audience and create a physical comprehensive guide for parents. We wanted to write a go-to resource that would cut through the confusion while also supporting a wholesome approach to eating.

And so, *Baby Food Bible* was born – the nourishing guide to feeding your family, from the very first bite and beyond. Our approach is simple because, truth be told, neither of us are chefs. We have embraced simplicity as our mantra because we understand the demands of having young children and we want to make feeding your family a joyous and uncomplicated experience. Our philosophy of 'food is medicine' is considered in every recipe.

But this book is not just the result of our efforts alone. It was through the incredible support of our beautiful online Bable community that *Baby Food Bible* truly came to life. They generously gave feedback, asked lots of questions and even tested our recipes on their families.

We'd like to invite you to also join us on this journey as we celebrate the joy of feeding the whole family and impart the knowledge and confidence we've gained to make healthy choices for your little one. Together, let's create meals that are not only nutritious, but also filled with love and the sheer delight of exploring the world of food with your baby.

Jules & Lauren x

A SOLID START

Congratulations! You and your little one have reached the important milestone of starting solid foods. You are likely feeling excited but perhaps also overwhelmed. There is so much to consider, so to help answer some of those questions, here are our top tips for starting solids:

+ Wait until your baby is developmentally ready before offering solid foods. The cues to look out for are outlined on page 10.
+ Do what's right for you and your baby. Don't worry about what everyone else is doing.
+ Let this be a time of sensory exploration for your baby.
+ Let your baby lead and trust they know when they're satisfied.
+ It's your job to provide, and their job to decide what they are going to eat.
+ Trust your gut. If you're concerned, speak to your healthcare provider.

SETTING UP SOLID FOUNDATIONS

WHEN TO START

Every child is unique and develops at their own pace. When it comes to introducing solid foods, it's crucial to tune in to your baby's individual developmental cues to determine when they are ready. Typically, the signs of readiness appear between 5.5 and 6.5 months. Introducing solids by 7 months is vital as your baby needs essential nutrients (that they can't obtain through breastmik and formula) to support their growth and development. If your baby hasn't displayed these signs by 7 months, we recommend seeking guidance from your healthcare provider.

The key indicators of readiness for starting solids are:

INDEPENDENT SITTING

Can your baby sit up on their own with minimal support? If so, this means their digestive muscles are sufficiently developed to handle solid foods.

HEAD AND NECK CONTROL

Can your baby hold their head upright and steady? This skill enables them to signal fullness by turning their head away when they've had enough and to reduce the risk of choking as they can keep their neck upright, ensuring their airway isn't narrowed.

INTEREST IN FOOD

Is your little one displaying curiosity about food, either by reaching for your meals or showing interest during mealtimes?

By waiting for these cues, you'll know your baby is developmentally ready.

FIRST TASTES

Starting solids is a significant milestone for you and your baby. Starting with simple, savoury wholefoods and working your way up to include a variety of seasonings is a great way to begin. This can help your little one become familiar with the taste of food in its most natural form before you try more exciting combinations. Blending foods with breastmilk or formula can provide a comforting and familiar taste, and ease the transition to solid foods.

We personally started our solids journeys spending a week or two offering tastes of simple, low-allergenic foods before getting more creative with combination purées and introducing a wider range of finger foods*. Some of our favourite first foods include avocado, banana, kidney beans or black beans, pumpkin, parsnip, sweet potato, beetroot (beet), zucchini (courgette), broccoli, carrot, cauliflower, peas, bone broth, chicken, lamb and beef.

You may choose to offer the same foods for a few days in a row, introduce new foods daily or offer a combination of foods together, but whatever you choose, know there's no right or wrong method. Embrace this exciting time exploring new tastes and flavours with your little one.

**We recommend a more staggered and mindful approach for introducing allergens (page 42).*

EASE INTO IT

Take your time and go at your and your baby's pace. Don't worry if you skip a day in the beginning or if your baby doesn't enjoy a certain food at first. It can take multiple exposures for them to develop a liking for it. Some days, they may be eager to try new foods, while other days they might show little interest.

EMBRACE THE MESS

When you start solids, the focus is on letting your baby explore food. As the old saying goes: 'Don't play with your food', but in this case, we say: *~~Don't~~ play with your food!* Let your little one feel it in their hands so they get comfortable with putting it in their mouth. It's important to allow them to discover not only different flavours but also different textures. In doing so, they will develop important skills like handling food with their mouths, using their hands and even trying out utensils.

This sensory experience may look like smearing purée all over their tray or squishing finger foods. So while you'll start finding food in unexpected places and your baby will likely be covered in mess, try to embrace the chaos and enjoy witnessing your little one discover the fun of food!

'~~DON'T~~ PLAY WITH YOUR FOOD!'

DINNER FOR BREAKFAST

When you first start introducing solid foods, your baby is not yet conditioned to understand the difference between breakfast, lunch, dinner and dessert. This means you can mix things up and introduce a variety of foods during their meals and offer more nutrient-dense options at any time of day. For example, it's perfectly okay to serve iron-rich lamb chops as part of their morning meal. Don't be afraid to break away from traditional expectations and let your little one explore different flavours and textures right from the start.

EXPANDING YOUR LITTLE ONE'S PALATE

It's important not to let your taste preferences impact what you feed your little one. Just because you don't favour a food, doesn't mean your baby won't. They have no prior experience or opinions about the food, meaning they are more likely to enjoy it. Some of the most nutritious foods are not the most popular ones with adults. We're talking sardines, sauerkraut, liver and tempeh. You might be surprised how much your little one takes to these flavours when starting their solids journey. Remember, they can't say yes to a food they haven't been offered so give it a go!

FLAVOURS, SEASONINGS AND SOUR FOODS

The first few months of solids is a great time to introduce a variety of flavours, especially before the fussy toddler days kick in. Adding just a little pinch of seasoning can broaden your baby's palate and set them up to become an adventurous eater. Herbs and spices also have a host of nutritional benefits so start adding them early on.

Introducing sour flavours at a young age is also beneficial for gut health and getting your baby used to unique flavours. In fact, eating sour foods can make your little one less prone to favouring sweet foods. Aim to include fermented foods like sauerkraut in their daily diet. It might just shock you how much they grow to love them!

WINDOW OF OPPORTUNITY

The window of opportunity is an important pocket of time to introduce variety and textures into your little one's diet. From approximately 6–9 months is the key time to offer varied textures, colours, flavours, be adventurous with herbs and spices, and limit the introduction of sweet and salty foods as much as possible. By making the most of this window, you can positively influence long-term eating habits.

YOU PROVIDE, YOUR BABY DECIDES

When it comes to mealtimes, focus on your role as the provider of food and let your child take charge of their role, which is listening to their body. First, let's ditch the pressure and expectations, whether it's by encouraging them to eat specific foods or insisting on eating a certain amount. Instead, let your baby follow their instincts. Your responsibility is to decide when and where meals happen, as well as what food options are available. It's up to your child, as an intuitive eater, to decide how much they eat or whether they eat at all. Trusting their innate body cues allows your child to develop a healthy relationship with food.

FAMILY MEALTIME

Mealtime with the family is where the magic happens. If you model that mealtime is a positive experience by actively enjoying your fruits and veggies, talking about the foods on offer and encouraging your little one to touch and smell the different foods, you will create a positive association with food that will hopefully last them a lifetime.

But it's not just about the food. Connecting as a family is also important so turn off the television, sit at the table and consider moving mealtime so the whole family can eat together (even if it's just a few times a week). Family mealtime requires patience and consistency, so it's important to try and set up these foundations from the get go.

TABLE TALK

When it comes to introducing solids, creating a positive and relaxed eating environment is key.

+ Set the mood by playing some music.
+ Sit together at the table and have a chat about your day or for those who can't talk yet, explain to them what's for dinner.
+ Limit distractions such as having the television on.
+ Encourage food exploration by modelling eating.
+ Give your baby freedom to eat and explore. Let them touch, smell and taste different foods. Food all over the floor is usually a sign of a successful mealtime!
+ If your little one starts getting grizzly or showing signs of disinterest, they've likely had enough and it's time to finish the meal.

TOOLS OF THE TRADE

Investing in a few key items will make your life so much easier when starting your little one on solids. We recommend:

+ A safe, comfortable and sturdy highchair with a footrest to promote good posture during mealtime.
+ Silicone bibs or smocks to protect their clothes from inevitable mess and you from unnecessary stress.
+ Suction bowls or plates to discourage the whole meal toppling onto the ground.
+ Silicone freezer pods to store and freeze homemade baby food in. This will make mealtime prep much more convenient.
+ Narrow silicone spoons, perfect for self-feeding. These can also be popped in the freezer for your baby to chew on when teething.

SPOON-FEEDING

Once you've got your head around signs of readiness, you'll need to decide what feeding method is right for you and your little one. If you're feeling anxious about finger foods, stick to spoon-feeding initially. A confident and relaxed parent is more important than starting finger foods before you and your baby are ready.

TEXTURE

Start with smooth and soup-like textures when introducing purées. Chunkier purées can sometimes trigger the gag reflex as babies are used to slurping their food like they do when breastfeeding or bottle feeding.

PROS	CONS
+ Easy to monitor how much your little one is eating. + Easy to make sure your little one is getting the right nutrients because you can combine certain nutrient-dense foods. + Able to prepare and freeze portions, meaning less food waste. + Mess is minimal because you're in control. + Some parents find starting with purées eases their anxiety about starting solids.	+ Easy to overfeed your little one. Overfeeding can lead to your baby wanting less breastmilk or formula, which is their primary source of nutrition until 12 months. + Does not encourage use of fine motor skills (but we do have a tip for this below). + Can make accepting new textures difficult. + Can be time-consuming to prepare separate meals to the rest of the family. + Your baby may develop a preference for softer textures.

SPOON TAG

Some babies have a knack for gripping tightly onto the spoon after taking a bite, leaving you in limbo while you're eager to load up the next spoonful. If this is your baby, try playing spoon tag. Have multiple spoons ready and preload one while your baby holds another. This playful game encourages independence and the development of fine motor skills.

PURÉE COMBOS

When making purées, try to include a combination of the following:

1. Iron- and zinc-rich foods such as meat, fish*, eggs*, chicken or legumes. These provide essential iron for healthy development.
2. Vegetables and fruits, as they contribute valuable micronutrients and carbohydrates to support overall nutrition.
3. Healthy fats, such as avocado or extra-virgin olive oil that aid in nutrient absorption, support satiety and assist in the prevention of constipation.
4. Flavours and seasonings to introduce different tastes, foster a sense of exploration and encourage an adventurous palate.

**Top allergens*

Chickpeas, butternut squash, zucchini (courgette), coconut cream, turmeric, pepper

Cannellini beans, beetroot (beet), bone broth, extra-virgin olive oil, paprika

Poached chicken, carrot, cauliflower, extra-virgin olive oil, turmeric

Baked chicken, pumpkin, cauliflower, extra-virgin olive oil, bone broth, garlic

LIQUIDS THAT CAN BE USED TO THIN A PURÉE INCLUDE:

+ Hug-in-a-cup broth (page 279)
+ Breastmilk or formula
+ Filtered water or water that has been boiled and cooled

BABY-LED WEANING

Baby-led weaning (BLW) means offering finger foods from the get go. Foods that are about the length of an adult finger are ideal for your baby to hold. This size allows them to have a portion that sticks out of their hand, making it easier for them to bite off small pieces safely. Stick-shaped foods are recommended for babies aged 6–9 months as they help them learn how much they can handle in their mouth. Once your baby has developed the pincer grasp (this usually happens around 9 months), you can introduce bite-sized pieces. For babies who are transitioning from purées to finger foods, it's still best to offer stick-shaped foods even if they have mastered their pincer grasp as this shape is safest to start with.

TEXTURE

Finger foods need to pass the squish test. Harder fruits and veggies such as apples, pears and carrots should be steamed or baked until they're soft enough to squish between your index finger and thumb. For younger babies, remove the peel as it can be difficult for them to break up and swallow. Softer fruits and vegetables like bananas, apricots and kiwi fruits can be offered raw. It can also be helpful to dip slippery finger foods into foods such as hemp seeds or desiccated coconut to help your little one grip them.

Meats such as lamb and beef are excellent first foods because they're high in iron. However, their chewy texture can cause parents some anxiety. When serving meat as a finger food make sure it's soft enough for your baby to chew. Slow cooking or poaching are great ways to ensure the meat has a soft texture (try our Slow-cooked lamb, page 237). Koftas are also a great option as babies can hold them and bite off little bits (try our Burger and chippies, page 241).

Chicken and fish should also be cooked until they're a soft texture (try our Chicken soup, page 213) or offered in stick-shaped pieces with any hidden bones carefully removed. The exceptions to the squish test are meat on the bone or chewy variations, such as steak. Steak should be well done and offered in larger pieces (the size of two adult fingers).

Give your baby some meat on the bone and let them have fun exploring it. For cuts like lamb cutlets and chicken drumsticks, the bone is a perfect handle for them to grasp. Just be sure to do a quick check and remove any loose gristle, skin and small bones before you serve it up.

If your little one does happen to bite off a large piece of meat, stay calm and let them work with the food in their mouth. If they ever need assistance in getting a piece of food out of their mouth, here's a handy tip: simply tilt them forward gently and place your hand beneath their chin. This gesture lets them know it's okay to spit it out.

PROS	CONS
+ Encourages motor skill development and independence. + Strengthens the gag reflex. + Exposes baby to a wider variety of textures, which may reduce picky eating down the track – this also makes it more fun! + Quick and easy to prepare – can be the same or a variation of the family meal. + Easier to include baby in the family mealtime and reap the benefits of motor and social skill development.	+ Can make carers anxious. + Can be more challenging to get in essential nutrients, such as iron, as serving foods like meat as a finger food can make carers anxious about choking. + Usually more food waste as food landing on the floor is less likely to be re-served. + Can be very messy but it's important to embrace the mess! + Difficult to know how much food has actually been eaten.

FUN WITH FINGER FOODS

Our goal for BLW (and solid foods in general) is to whip up one dish for the entire family, which can be easily adapted for little foodies-in-training.

1. Burger (made into koftas)* and chippies (page 241)
2. Baked potato with a smear of purée
3. Preloaded spoon of purée (let your baby feed themselves as part of combo-feeding – page 24)
4. Ripe avocado spear coated in hemp seeds
5. Sauerkraut in a self-feeder
6. Slow-cooked lamb (page 237)
7. Supercharged squishies sliced into stick-shaped pieces (page 172)
8. Shredded Roast chook (page 206)
9. Crinkle-cut steamed carrot drizzled with coconut oil and cinnamon
10. Cauliflower with extra-virgin olive oil and cumin
11. Kiwi fruit spear
12. Steamed pear with coconut oil and cinnamon
13. Tinned sardine* – rinsed and bones squished – with a squeeze of lemon
14. Baked sweet potato with a smear of purée
15. Speedy spinach omelette (page 110)
16. Grilled zucchini (courgette) spear with extra-virgin olive oil and cumin, and a yoghurt dip
17. Steamed broccoli floret with extra-virgin olive oil
18. Lamb cutlet pan-fried in ghee* and seasoned with rosemary (remove any gristle and loose fat)
19. Chicken drumstick cooked in extra-virgin olive oil and seasoned with lemon and thyme (remove any gristle and small bones)
20. Banana halved or chopped into a spear and sprinkled with cinnamon

1

4

5

10

14

18

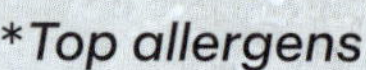

Top allergens

3
2
7
8
9
6
12
11
13
16
17
15
20
19

COMBO-FEEDING

Combo-feeding means a combination of offering purées and finger foods. It's a fantastic way to encourage self-feeding, which helps your baby hone their motor skills. When it comes to offering purées, a handy tip is to preload the spoon for your baby and then pass it to them so they can practice self-feeding. Make sure to try this before they reach 9 months old to ensure the window of opportunity is not missed.

PROS	CONS
+ Offering a combination of purées and finger foods allows your baby to experience different textures and tastes. + Ensures your baby receives a diverse range of nutrients from both purées and finger foods. + Supports development of motor skills and self-feeding. + Exposes your baby to a wide variety of textures. + Can be helpful in the transition period from purées to finger foods.	+ From a motor-skill perspective, your baby may be confused when transitioning between spoon-feeding and self-feeding. For example, sucking purée from a spoon is a different skill to chewing on finger foods. + Less of an opportunity to practice appetite control.

PURÉES AS DIPS

Who says purées have to be confined to boring old spoons? Think outside of the bowl and transform those purées into finger-food dips, or even smear some purée onto the finger foods for them to explore.

GAGGING VS. CHOKING

Choking and gagging may be front of mind when starting your little one on solids. But do you know the differences between them?

GAGGING

+ Can be quite noisy and dramatic – resembles coughing or retching.
+ Serves as a protective mechanism to prevent large objects from entering the airway: it's a natural reflex.
+ Considered normal and safe as it helps babies learn about the size and shape of food for safe swallowing.
+ Typically decreases over time as your little one becomes a more experienced eater.
+ No intervention is needed: stay calm, take a deep breath and let your baby practice pushing the food out of their mouth on their own.

CHOKING

+ Is completely *silent*.
+ Indicates that something is obstructing the airway.
+ Immediate intervention* is vital to clear the airway and restore normal breathing.

**We recommend all parents or caregivers undertake a CPR course to gain confidence around mealtimes and ensure they're well equipped to confidently respond in an emergency.*

CHOKING HAZARDS

While there are lots of fantastic finger foods, some need more careful consideration. For example, remember to remove pits when offering stone fruits and chop up hard foods like apples and carrots into safe pieces or serve them cooked instead. Cherry tomatoes, grapes and blueberries can pose a choking risk when served whole so refer to page 27 for preparation instructions.

TIPS TO MINIMISE THE RISK OF CHOKING

+ Always offer foods seated at the table under supervision.
+ No food in the car.
+ If offering any of the following foods, ensure they're prepared and modified appropriately.

MODIFICATIONS FOR HIGHER-RISK FOODS

	HOW TO SERVE/MODIFY				
FOOD	**6 MO +**	**9 MO +**	**12 MO +**	**18 MO +**	**24 MO +**
CHERRY TOMATOES	Avoid	Quarter		Halve	
GRAPES	Avoid	Quarter		Halve	
BLUEBERRIES	Purée or flatten/squish	Flatten/squish or quarter		Offer whole*	
CHICKPEAS & PEAS	Purée or mash	Flatten/ squish	Offer whole		
APPLES	Cooked and halved or as a purée	Thin slices		Whole but partially peeled	Quartered*
CARROTS	Cooked and cut lengthwise or as a purée	Cooked and cut into bite-sized pieces or raw, serve grated		Raw and served as sticks	Offer whole*
NUTS AND SEEDS	Smooth butters or finely ground and sprinkled onto other foods		Butters spread on toast or finger foods		Split nuts in half lengthwise* and offer seed butters or whole seeds*

***This will depend on your child's eating ability. When your little one is showing mature chewing skills, they can progress to the food in this form.**

MEALTIME CHECKLIST

Whether your little one has just started solids or is an active toddler, this checklist will help you make mealtime safe and stress free.

+ Always have your little one sitting upright in a highchair or booster seat during mealtimes – avoid reclining or lying down positions.
+ Keep a close eye on your baby while they are eating. Avoid all distractions like having the television on or looking at your phone.
+ Make sure foods are a safe size, shape and are age appropriate. We have specific guidelines for purées on page 17 and BLW on page 20.
+ Ensure your baby is in control. If practising BLW, allow your baby to have complete control over the food that goes into their mouth and comes out.
+ Never remove food from your baby's mouth if they are gagging. Allow the gag reflex to do its job.

HOW MUCH AND HOW OFTEN?

It can be really confusing knowing how often and how much to feed your baby. Unfortunately, there's no one-size-fits-all answer. Instead, we've put together a general guide to help you, noting it's important to try to follow your baby's cues. Say goodbye to adult expectations that we should polish off everything on our plates. Instead, start with small quantities and offer more if your baby shows interest.

Some babies may be keen for more food very quickly, while others will take it slow. Some days your baby may not be interested in food and barely eat a thing; other days they might want *more, more, more*!

If you're concerned about your baby gaining weight, focus on milk feeds primarily* and check in with your healthcare provider.

**For babies under 12 months.*

SNACKS

Offering snacks is not necessary before 12 months. Instead, focus on increasing the frequency of meals and how much you are serving if you feel your little one needs more food during the day.

If your baby isn't eating what you consider 'much', prioritise offering nutrient-dense foods. In the early months it's important that these foods are rich in iron and zinc as these are key nutrients for their growth and development that can't be met with milk feeds alone.

6–7 MONTHS

Begin introducing solids by offering one meal a day. One meal may look like 1–2 tablespoons of purée or a couple of pieces of finger food.

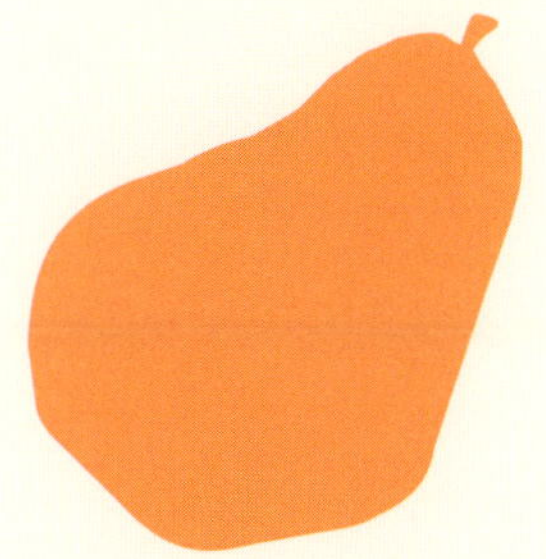

7–9 MONTHS

Increase the frequency to two meals a day. These meals may increase slightly to ¼ cup or ⅓ cup of purée or a few more pieces of finger food.

9–12 MONTHS

If your baby shows interest by 9 months, you can offer up to three meals a day. (By 12 months, they should be having three meals.) At 9 months, they should predominantly be eating finger foods. Start by offering a few pieces and continue offering until they indicate they've had enough.

12 MONTHS+ (TODDLERHOOD)

Continue offering three meals a day and start introducing snacks between meals if your little one is interested. Be mindful of snacks falling too close to mealtime or too many snacks replacing main meals.

FULLNESS CUES

When your baby is full, they will tell you. Although they likely can't tell you with words yet, don't worry they will make themselves very clear! It's important not to pressure your baby to eat. There's no need to count bites or sneak in extra spoonfuls. Respect your baby's signs of fullness and tune in to their cues to pre-empt mealtime meltdowns.

On the flipside, if your baby is not yet full they will also give you signs.

SIGNS YOUR BABY IS FULL MAY INCLUDE:

+ Turning their head away from the spoon or displaying disinterest.
+ Hitting the spoon or throwing their food.
+ Changing their facial expression from concentration to mischievous.
+ Becoming frustrated or upset (this can also happen if they are too hungry or tired).
+ Playing with their food more than eating it.
+ Shifting in their seat and showing a desire to get out.

SIGNS YOUR BABY WANTS MORE FOOD MAY INCLUDE:

+ Pointing
+ Grabbing at food
+ Asking for more (if they have started talking). You can keep offering food until your baby makes it clear they're full.

BREASTMILK, FORMULA AND OTHER LIQUIDS

BREASTMILK OR FORMULA

Breastmilk or formula should be your little one's primary source of nutrition until 12 months. Therefore, it's important that your baby doesn't fill up on solids or other liquids and refuse their milk feeds. To avoid this, make sure to offer milk before solids until 12 months. If you notice your baby refusing their milk feeds, rather than gradually weaning, pull back on solids and other liquids to balance this out.

INTRODUCING WATER AND OTHER LIQUIDS

As soon as your little one starts solids, small sips of boiled and cooled water or Hug-in-a-cup broth (page 279) can be slowly introduced as well. When meals increase, their water intake can increase to match accordingly. While breastmilk or formula will be the main source of hydration until 12 months, these complementary liquids can help prevent constipation.

Small open cups are a great vehicle for liquids as they help develop fine motor skills. We also recommend offering a straw. You may need to model how to use this a few times, but it's a great way for your baby to practise their sucking skills.

COW'S MILK

A common misconception is that your little one needs to transition to cow's milk after their first birthday to replace either breastmilk or formula. Another misconception is that cow's milk is needed to reach their daily calcium needs. While cow's milk is a great source of calcium among other things, it certainly isn't the only source, nor our first choice. Nutritionally, children do not require cow's milk as a replacement and can reach their calcium needs through other dietary sources (page 50).

Here are a few reasons why cow's milk isn't our drink of choice:

+ Too much cow's milk (>500 ml/ >17 fl oz/2 cups per day) can inhibit iron absorption.
+ It's very filling and may impact your baby's intake of solids.
+ The protein found in cow's milk can be harder to digest for babies due to their immature digestive system.

Instead, we recommend meeting calcium and other nutritional needs through a wholefoods diet. If your little one relies on a bottle for comfort after 12 months, you could offer water, bone broth or cooled herbal tea, such as chamomile, in a sippy cup or drink bottle.

PROCESSED BABY FOODS

The baby food aisle can be very appealing to time-poor parents. We get it – it's the epitome of convenience! Unfortunately just because a baby food product is marketed as containing fruits, vegetables or even iron, it doesn't mean it's a healthy choice.

BABY CEREAL

Baby cereal is an ultra-processed food, made up predominantly of refined rice flour. During the processing methods, most vitamins and minerals are removed, leaving it void of key nutrients your little one requires at this pivotal age of development.

Here are a few reasons why we don't recommend baby cereal:

+ Baby cereal is fortified with synthetic iron, which can be harder for babies to absorb and digest and can lead to constipation.
+ The bland taste and lack of flavour does not encourage the development of adventurous eating.
+ It doesn't contain other essential nutrients babies need such as healthy fats, calcium, vitamin D, choline and naturally occurring iron.
+ There is arsenic present in the rice flour. Arsenic, a heavy metal, is absorbed into our rice crops through the environment and subsequently ingested by our little ones. (We talk more about heavy metals on page 74.)

BABY FOOD POUCHES

To ensure these products are shelf stable for a long time, many baby food pouches are heavily processed under ultra-high heat, voiding them of lots of key nutrients. This processing leaves an end-product that is far from its original source. For instance, with the dietary fibre removed, it's hard for your little one to feel signs of fullness or satiety.

Children need to see foods in their whole form to learn to like them. It's also important your baby sees the foods they are eating to self-regulate their appetite. Pouches are easy to suck on so it's easy for babies to finish the pouch without registering whether they're full. What's the alternative to baby cereal and food pouches? Wholefoods!

Offering a diet rich in wholefoods, 'real food' oozing with the key vitamins and minerals their bodies require, starts in the fresh produce aisles of the supermarket. Think meat, fish, poultry, nuts and seeds, wholegrains, legumes and, of course, fresh fruit and vegetables.

Their little tummies and digestive systems are still maturing, so food in its purest form is so much more beneficial to them to help establish their immune system, build a healthy strong gut microbiome and ultimately to help them thrive! And what if we told you offering a wide variety of colours, textures and flavours could make your little one less picky later. Most of the processed purée options taste very sweet and are puréed rather than in their 'real food' form, meaning your little one's palate may not be as adventurous or well-rounded down the track.

We're not saying there isn't a time and place for convenient baby food snacks, sachets and pouches. But it's important at this crucial stage of development that these foods are not your baby's primary source of nutrition, rather a 'sometimes food' offered in moderation in combination with a wholefoods diet.

'CHILDREN NEED TO SEE FOODS IN THEIR WHOLE FORM TO LEARN TO LIKE THEM.'

MAKING SENSE OF SODIUM

Sodium is a naturally occurring mineral found in many of the foods we eat, including veggies, meat, eggs, breastmilk and formula. It plays a vital role in your little one's bodily functions. However, it's important to limit foods with excessive sodium as consuming too much sodium can increase blood pressure, which is a primary risk factor for long-term chronic disease.

Unfortunately in Western society with the rise of ultra-processed packaged foods, children are consuming much more sodium than recommended. Too much sodium can also impact your little one's taste preferences, so we recommend avoiding adding salt to their food before 12 months. Having said that, don't fret if your baby has small amounts of salted food from time to time.

Once your little one reaches 12 months, a pinch of salt (we recommend natural sea salt) in meals is okay, but be mindful of limiting processed foods with high sodium levels. For example, too much cheddar cheese, feta, haloumi, bacon, canned beans, soy sauce and tomato sauce with your salty chippies – you get the idea. Instead, prioritise wholefoods. We're big on seasoning but instead of salt, try fresh or dried herbs and spices (we have some seasoning ideas on page 38).

SMART SODIUM SWAPS

HIGH-SODIUM FOODS	SWAPS
Cheeses such as haloumi, feta and cheddar	Cottage cheese, ricotta, fresh mozzarella/bocconcini, Swiss cheese
Soy sauce and tamari	Coconut aminos
Tomato sauce	Tomato passata
Deli meats	Homemade roast meats
Canned beans and legumes	Dried beans and legumes or rinse canned beans before consuming
Stock	Hug-in-a-cup (page 279)
Pre-packaged snacks*	Try our recipes instead!

**For a low-sodium option, aim for less than 120 mg/100 g (3½ oz) and for a medium–low sodium option, aim for less than 400 mg/100 g (3½ oz).*

MAKING SENSE OF SUGAR

Sugar is a type of carbohydrate that provides energy to your cells. Sugar can naturally be found in foods (intrinsic/natural sugars), or it can be added through the food-manufacturing process (added sugars and/or refined sugars). While both types of sugars are metabolised in the body the same way, not all sugar is created equal so it's important to pay attention to the quality of sugar you're offering your little one.

'NOT ALL SUGAR IS CREATED EQUAL.'

The difference between refined sugar and natural sugar is that refined sugar has gone through heavy processing, stripping the food of vitamins, minerals and, most importantly, fibre. Natural sugar, on the other hand, is found naturally in food. It has not undergone processing so all the vitamins and minerals are intact.

When buying packaged foods, be mindful of added or hidden sugars. A low-sugar option is less than 5–10 g/100 g (3½ oz), or 5000–10000 mg (3½ oz). Sugar is hidden in the majority of manufactured products so it's important to always read the ingredients list.

A baby's taste preferences are highly influenced by the foods they consume from an early age. When offering your little one sugary foods on a regular basis, not only does their body crave more of it but their taste preferences begin to change. Introducing refined sugars from an early age is a contributing factor for children developing fussy eating behaviours. We recommend avoiding refined and added sugars altogether in your baby's first year of life.

Instead, we love to sweeten our baked goods naturally with sweet fruits such as overripe bananas, berries or puréed apples. Alternatively, our Date paste (page 268) is a fantastic alternative to refined sugar. Our added sugars of choice are maple syrup and high-quality honey (for babies over 12 months), as even though they are 'added' to the food, they are less processed and therefore have a better nutrient profile.

While we recommend avoiding sugary options, like everything, balance is important and the overarching goal is to help your child develop a good relationship with food in the long term. For example, at a party it's equally important to not stop your child from enjoying those treats everyone else is grabbing. We believe in making healthy decisions at home and taking a more relaxed approach when we're out. It's what you do most of the time – not some of the time – that matters!

SEASONING

Rather than relying on sugar or salt for flavour, here are some of our favourite food and seasoning pairings that the whole family will enjoy.

1. **PARSLEY**
   - + Eggs
   - + Fish or chicken

2. **FENNEL SEEDS**
   - + Fish
   - + Tomato-based sauces

3. **CORIANDER (CILANTRO)**
   - + Avocado, corn, sweet potato or broccoli
   - + Black beans

4. **CUMIN SEEDS**
   - + Lamb, beef, pork or chicken
   - + Carrot or beetroot (beet)

5. **TURMERIC**
   - + Carrot or cauliflower
   - + Rice or quinoa

6. **PEPPERCORNS**
   - + Add a crack of black pepper to all turmeric dishes to improve the bioavailability

7. **THYME**
   - + Parsnip, carrot or potato
   - + Chicken or beef

8. **LEMON**
   - + Fish or shellfish
   - + Ricotta or goat's cheese
   - + Blueberries or blackberries

9. **VANILLA BEAN**
   - + Coconut, mango or banana

10. **OREGANO**
    - + Chicken, fish, seafood or pork
    - + Tomato-based sauces

11. **GARLIC**
    - + Lentils or tempeh
    - + Beef or chicken

12. **BASIL**
    - + Tomato or artichoke

13. **PAPRIKA**
    - + Pumpkin (squash) or carrot
    - + Chicken or eggs

14. **MINT**
    - + Watermelon
    - + Peas
    - + Lamb

15. **ROSEMARY**
    - + Butternut squash or mushrooms
    - + Lamb, pork, steak or fish

16. **CINNAMON**
    - + Apple, banana or blueberries
    - + Sweet potato
    - + Oats and yoghurt

17. **ONION POWDER**
    - + Beef or chicken
    - + Roasted veggies

2
3
4
10
9
8
14
13
15
16
17

FOOD ALLERGENS

Once you've mastered some basic first foods, it's important to start introducing allergens. We're both parents so we get it – trialling allergens can be nerve-racking.

When introducing new foods to your child, it's important to be aware of potential reactions and know how to respond. Allergy symptoms can occur within minutes or up to 2 hours after an exposure. However, an immediate reaction makes it easier to identify the specific food causing the response.

Our goal is to empower you with the knowledge and tools to safely navigate the introduction of allergenic foods and manage any reactions that may occur. If your baby does have an allergy or food sensitivity, we've also included some alternatives to common allergenic foods.

HOW TO INTRODUCE THE TOP 9 ALLERGENS

The Top 9 allergens are egg, peanut, tree nuts, sesame, fish, shellfish, soy, dairy and wheat. When introducing these foods, we recommend:

OFFERING LOW-RISK FOODS FIRST

Do not offer allergens as the first solid foods.

MAKING SURE YOUR BABY IS IN GOOD HEALTH

It's important to refrain from introducing allergenic foods when your baby is unwell because their immune system may be compromised, making them more susceptible to potential reactions.

BEING EXTRA CAUTIOUS WITH HIGH-RISK BABIES

If your baby is at a higher risk of developing allergies – for instance, if they have a family history of allergies or existing conditions like moderate to severe eczema, asthma or other food allergies – consult with your paediatrician or allergist before introducing allergenic foods. They may recommend allergy testing or a modified introduction plan.

STARTING SMALL AND GRADUALLY INCREASING

Begin with small amounts of an allergenic food, approximately a quarter of a teaspoon, and gradually increase the quantity at each exposure if there are no adverse reactions.

INTRODUCING ALLERGENS EARLY IN THE DAY AND OBSERVING YOUR BABY CLOSELY

Most allergic reactions occur within 2 hours of ingestion. To ensure a safer introduction, introduce allergens during your baby's mid-morning wake window when they are generally in a good mood and less likely to be overtired. This also allows you ample time to look for any adverse reactions before their nap and respond appropriately if needed.

TESTING FOR ALLERGENS AT HOME

Offer allergenic foods at home rather than in a cafe, at someone else's house or while on holiday.

INTRODUCING ALLERGENS ONE AT A TIME

This approach helps you pinpoint the specific food responsible for an adverse response. Symptoms may not appear immediately and it can take a few introductions before they become detectable.

WHEAT
SESAME
EGG
DAIRY
TREE NUTS
SOY
FISH
PEANUTS
SHELLFISH

HOW OFTEN?

To determine if your little one has any allergies, introduce each allergenic food separately, leaving about 4 days between each exposure. This approach allows you to observe if they have a reaction to a specific food more easily. It may take a couple of tries before any reaction becomes noticeable, so offer the allergenic food a few times over a 2-week period, carefully observing your child after each exposure.

For example, let's say you offer peanuts. Wait 4 days and if there's no reaction, offer peanuts again. Then wait another 4 days and if there's still no reaction, offer peanuts one more time. Wait 4 days and if there's still no signs of allergy or sensitivity, great! You can now safely include peanuts in their regular diet and move on to introducing a new allergenic food.

REGULAR EXPOSURE IS KEY!

Once an allergenic food has been successfully introduced, make sure to incorporate it into your baby's diet a couple of times per week. Regular exposure, even in small amounts, can help prevent allergies.

TOP TIP

Observe your child for 2 hours after offering an allergen. If your child experiences an allergic reaction, see opposite for how to proceed.

HOW TO SPOT AN ALLERGIC REACTION

MILD OR MODERATE REACTIONS

SYMPTOMS OF MILD TO MODERATE REACTIONS COMMONLY INCLUDE:

+ Hives
+ Mild facial rash
+ Reddening of the skin (without swelling)
+ Tingling/itching in the mouth.

HOW TO PROCEED

+ Stop the meal and remove the food.
+ Clean up and wipe their hands and face to minimise further exposure.
+ Stay with your child and watch for any signs of swelling or lethargy.
+ DO NOT reintroduce that food and contact a healthcare provider for further guidance.

SEVERE REACTIONS

SYMPTOMS OF SEVERE REACTIONS COMMONLY INCLUDE:

+ Swelling in the face, throat or mouth
+ Throat tightening
+ Difficulty breathing
+ Severe wheezing
+ Abdominal pain
+ Immediate vomiting
+ Anaphylactic reactions (weakness, floppiness, lethargy, drowsiness, loss of consciousness).

HOW TO PROCEED

CALL AN AMBULANCE IMMEDIATELY.

DO NOT reintroduce that food and contact a healthcare provider for future guidance.

DELAYED REACTIONS

If symptoms appear after 2 hours or up to 3 days later, it's likely to be a sensitivity or intolerance, as opposed to an allergy. We recommend speaking to your healthcare provider for further guidance.

ALLERGEN MASTER GUIDE

ALLERGEN	WHAT TO INTRODUCE	HOW TO INTRODUCE (PURÉE)	HOW TO INTRODUCE (BLW)
EGG	Egg yolk	Mix soft-boiled yolk into a purée your baby tolerates well.	Fry an egg yolk then slice it into strips.
	Whole egg	Stir an egg through a purée while cooking until it becomes creamy.	Fry an egg then slice it into strips.
PEANUTS	Peanuts and peanut butter	Mix smooth natural peanut butter into a purée your baby tolerates or offer on its own thinned to desired consistency with coconut oil.	Thinly smear a small amount of peanut butter on a finger food.
TREE NUTS	Almonds, walnuts, pecans, cashews, macadamia nuts, pistachio nuts, chestnuts, hazelnuts, shea nuts, Brazil nuts and pine nuts (individually)	Mix smooth natural nut butter or nut flour such as almond meal into a purée your baby tolerates or offer on its own thinned to desired consistency with coconut oil.	Thinly smear a small amount of nut butter on a finger food.
SESAME	Sesame seeds, sesame oil, hulled tahini	Mix smooth tahini into a purée your baby tolerates or offer on its own thinned to desired consistency with coconut oil.	Thinly smear a small amount of tahini on a finger food or add a sprinkle of sesame seeds.
FISH	White fish such as sardines, mackerel, snapper, barramundi, whiting (tinned or cooked)	Blend fish into a purée your baby tolerates and thin to desired consistency with bone broth, breastmilk or formula.	Offer rinsed tinned sardines.
SOY	Edamame, tempeh, tofu and soy milk	Blend edamame or tempeh into puréed baby food or thin to desired consistency with bone broth, breastmilk or formula.	Offer cooked tempeh in stick-shaped pieces or squished edamame.

QUALITY CONSIDERATIONS	NOTES
Certified organic and pasture-raised eggs contain the highest levels of DHA, a critical nutrient for your baby's developing brain. Pasture-raised eggs have the highest level of vitamin D.	High-risk babies should start with egg yolk as the yolk is less allergenic and then introduce egg whites as part of the whole egg. Always ensure eggs are cooked through.
	Introduce egg whites once egg yolk is tolerated. Ensure they're cooked through.
Choose natural smooth peanut butter without sugar, salt, seed oils or other additives.	Rub a small amount of peanut butter on the inside of baby's lip. If there is no reaction after a few minutes, proceed with offering more.
Choose nut butters without sugar, salt, seed oils or other additives.	Rub a small amount of your chosen nut butter on the inside of baby's lip. If there is no reaction after a few minutes, proceed with offering more. Some people are only allergic to one variety of tree nut but are fine with others so it's important to be cautious and test each nut individually.
Choose hulled tahini for a creamier consistency.	Rub a small amount of tahini on the inside of baby's lip. If using whole sesame seeds, crush them slightly to ensure they're fully digested for the purpose of allergen exposure.
Choose wild-caught fish and low-mercury options. For tinned fish, opt for wild caught in olive oil or water and BPA-free tins.	All fish species are different. However, if your baby is allergic to one species of fish, the recommendation is to avoid all fish. Avoid salmon, tuna and halibut for initial fish introduction.
Choose organic soy products to avoid GMOs.	

ALLERGEN	WHAT TO INTRODUCE	HOW TO INTRODUCE (PURÉE)	HOW TO INTRODUCE (BLW)
SHELLFISH	Crustaceans: Shrimp, prawns, crab, crayfish, lobster	Blend well-cooked shellfish such as shrimp with puréed baby food or thin to desired consistency with bone broth, breastmilk or formula.	Smear a small amount of purée on finger foods. Alternatively cut shrimp or prawn in half lengthways.
	Molluscs: Oysters mussels, scallops and clams	Blend pre-cooked canned oysters with puréed baby food or thin to desired consistency with bone broth, breastmilk or formula.	Smear a small amount of oyster or mussel purée on a finger food.
DAIRY	Ghee, butter, milk kefir and natural yoghurt	Mix ghee or butter with puréed baby food. Once well tolerated, offer natural yoghurt or kefir.	Cook finger food of choice in butter or ghee. Once well tolerated, dip finger foods in natural yoghurt or kefir.
WHEAT	Whole-wheat bread or sourdough and whole-wheat pasta.	Blend a whole-wheat flour into a purée they tolerate well.	Offer 100% whole-wheat pasta or sourdough large ends of thick bread, about the size of two adult fingers held together.
BELOW ARE A FEW OTHER FOODS THAT ARE NOT TOP 9 ALLERGENS BUT ARE WORTH BEING AWARE OF:			

GLUTEN

Gluten is not considered a common allergen. While some individuals have a medical condition called celiac disease or non-celiac gluten sensitivity that requires them to avoid gluten, most people can consume gluten without any adverse effects and without the potential risk of causing anaphylaxis.

HONEY

While not an allergen, you should completely avoid honey until your baby is 12 months old. Honey can contain a bacterium that causes infantile botulism – a rare but extremely serious form of food poisoning. Honey is a natural sweetener so can be enjoyed in moderation from 12 months onwards.

QUALITY CONSIDERATIONS	NOTES
For tinned options, look for an olive oil or water base and BPA-free tins.	Only offer shellfish in age-appropriate shapes and sizes to minimise choking risk. Always ensure shellfish is well cooked to avoid food poisoning. Commonly, if you are allergic to one type of shellfish, you're more likely to be allergic to the other types of shellfish in that group.
Choose organic, unflavoured and full fat varieties.	Delay the introduction of cow's milk until 12 months. The introduction of cheese is also preferable after 12 months due to its high-sodium content.
Choose organic where possible and avoid additives and preservatives.	Those who have a wheat allergy might still be able to consume other grains that contain gluten. However, those who have a gluten intolerance should steer clear of all grains that contain gluten.

CITRUS FRUITS

Citrus fruits can sometimes cause nappy (diaper) rash or rashes around a baby's mouth due to the fruit's acidity. While some younger babies may handle citrus fruits well, many babies can't tolerate them until 10–12 months. You don't need to treat citrus fruits with the same level of caution as top allergens, but it's still a good idea to approach them mindfully and watch out for possible reactions.

ALLERGEN SWAPS

If your baby has an allergy, sensitivity or food intolerance, there are lots of substitutions you can try. It's crucial to ensure that your baby's nutritional needs are met when avoiding specific foods or a food group due to allergies or other reasons. These substitutions aim to provide alternatives, but it's essential to consider your baby's nutritional requirements and consult a healthcare provider when managing allergies or dietary restrictions.

COW'S DAIRY

MILK SWAPS

+ Nut or seed milks such as almond milk, hemp milk or cashew milk
+ Coconut milk
+ Oat milk
+ Soy milk.

YOGHURT AND CREAM SWAPS

+ Coconut yoghurt
+ Soy yoghurt
+ Coconut cream
+ Silken tofu.

CHEESE SWAPS

+ Cashew cheese
+ Nutritional yeast.

BUTTER SWAPS

+ Use extra-virgin olive oil or coconut oil in baking and cooking.
+ Try avocado, coconut butter or nut or seed butters.

EGGS

THESE BINDERS REPLACE ONE EGG

+ Mix 1 tablespoon of chia seeds and 3 tablespoons of water together and let the mixture stand for 5–20 minutes.
+ Mash up half a medium-sized banana.
+ Make 'flax egg' by mixing 1 tablespoon of ground linseed (flax seed) and 3 tablespoons of warm water and let the mixture stand for 15 minutes.
+ Use half a cup of puréed apple sauce.
+ Mix 1 tablespoon of grass-fed gelatin and 2 tablespoons of cold water and allow the mixture to bloom for 2 minutes.
+ Add 3 tablespoons of aquafaba.
+ Mix 2 tablespoons of arrowroot flour and 3 tablespoons of water together.

FISH AND SHELLFISH

FISH AND SHELLFISH SWAPS

+ Focus on other animal proteins such as eggs, poultry and meat.

SOY

EDAMAME SWAPS

+ Try lentils, quinoa or other beans.

SOY MILK SWAPS

+ Nut or seed milks such as almond milk, hemp milk or cashew milk
+ Coconut milk
+ Oat milk.

TOFU AND TEMPEH SWAPS

+ Legumes such as beans, chickpeas and lentils
+ Mushrooms.

Use coconut aminos instead of soy sauce.

WHEAT AND GLUTEN

FLOUR SWAPS

+ Ground almond meal or almond flour
+ Besan (chickpea flour)
+ Buckwheat flour
+ Quinoa flour
+ Millet flour
+ Certified gluten-free oat flour
+ Brown rice flour
+ Coconut flour
+ Sorghum flour
+ Tapioca flour.

PEANUTS

PEANUT BUTTER SWAPS

+ Seed butters – our favourites are sunflower or pepita (pumpkin seed) and tahini.
+ Nut butters – our favourites are almond or cashew.

TREE NUTS

TREE NUT BUTTER SWAPS

+ Seed butters – our favourites are sunflower or pepita (pumpkin seed) and tahini.

TREE NUT MEAL/FLOUR SWAPS

+ Ground linseed (flax seed)
+ Besan (chickpea flour)
+ Coconut flour
+ Spelt flour
+ Oat flour
+ Wheat flour
+ Sunflower seed flour.

SESAME

TAHINI SWAPS

+ Peanut butter
+ Nut butters such as almond or cashew.

NOURISHING YOUR LITTLE ONE

Our philosophy centres around 'food is medicine' and the greatest foods are *wholefoods*. Wholefoods are made up of vitamins, minerals, antioxidants and phytochemicals – and these super-powerful elements support immunity, create energy, help to heal infections and wounds, and fight against disease.

From the moment your little one has their first mouthful of solid food, there is so much you can do to support their health and development – both in the short and long term.

Focus on feeding your little one wholefoods, which are foods that come as close to their natural state as possible, and limit processed and packaged foods. In fact, we recommend the whole family follows this approach.

While being mindful of what you're feeding your baby is important, don't let food drive you crazy. Try not to be too calculated about everything that goes into their mouth and don't let the mum guilt we all experience get you down. Knowledge is power and we're here to break it down for you and take the guesswork out, and provide nutritionally considered, beautifully balanced and delicious recipes that your little one will love (yes, even the fussy ones).

ESSENTIAL NUTRIENTS

IRON

Iron is an essential mineral, meaning your body does not make it, rather it needs to be obtained through diet. It's needed to produce haemoglobin, allowing red blood cells to effectively transport oxygen around the body. Iron is crucial for the growth and development of your baby's brain and cognition.

Babies are born with iron reserves from their mother's blood, which will last until approximately 6 months of age. From then, they need to consume enough iron-rich foods to avoid iron deficiency and anaemia. Between 6–24 months, your baby's iron requirements are the highest at any point in their life.

Iron deficiency can impact a child's growth, lead to behavioural issues, cognitive delay, learning difficulties, poor concentration, higher susceptibility to infections and fatigue.

'BETWEEN 6–24 MONTHS, YOUR BABY'S IRON REQUIREMENTS ARE THE HIGHEST AT ANY POINT IN THEIR LIFE.'

Iron can be obtained from haem (animal) sources or non-haem (plant-based) sources. Haem sources are more easily absorbed by the body, up to 35 per cent absorption, while non-haem iron is only absorbed from 2 to 13 per cent.

By pairing vitamin C with non-haem iron-rich foods, absorption is increased by up to three times.

RICH SOURCES OF HAEM IRON INCLUDE:

+ Organ meats such as liver
+ Oysters
+ Tinned sardines and tuna
+ Grass-fed beef
+ Wild-caught salmon
+ Lamb
+ Eggs
+ Chicken.

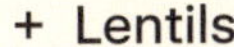

RICH SOURCES OF NON-HAEM IRON INCLUDE:

+ Lentils
+ Quinoa
+ Beans (kidney, white beans, navy, pinto, black, adzuki and lima)
+ Tinned tomatoes
+ Asparagus
+ Spinach
+ Chickpeas
+ Tofu
+ Potatoes
+ Snow peas (mange tout)
+ Dried apricots
+ Sesame/tahini
+ Pepitas (pumpkin seeds)
+ Nuts (almonds, cashews, hazelnuts, macadamia nuts and pistachios)
+ Kale
+ Peas.

FOODS RICH IN VITAMIN C THAT INCREASE ABSORPTION INCLUDE:

+ Peas
+ Broccoli
+ Cabbage
+ Cauliflower
+ Spinach
+ Tomatoes
+ Brussels sprouts
+ Sauerkraut
+ Kiwi fruits
+ Berries
+ Citrus fruits such as oranges, lemons and grapefruit.

SOME SIMPLE COMBINATIONS TO INCREASE YOUR LITTLE ONE'S IRON INTAKE INCLUDE:

+ Add kale, spinach, hemp seeds, linseed (flax seed) and chia seeds to a smoothie.
+ Add kale or spinach to an omelette or scrambled eggs.
+ Add liver powder to bolognese.
+ Add chia seeds, hemp seeds or ground linseed (flax seed) to porridge.
+ Sprinkle ground linseed (flax seed) or hemp seeds on spears of avocado and banana.
+ Replace wheat pasta with legume-based pulse pasta.
+ Add dried apricots to lunchboxes.
+ Offer a form of vitamin C on the plate with non-haem iron-rich foods. Add fruits such as berries, kiwi fruit, oranges or a squeeze of lemon.

RECIPES RICH IN IRON INCLUDE:

+ Meatballs and veggie sauce (page 234)
+ Cheesy broccoli bombs (page 200)
+ Crunchy seed snaps (page 155)
+ Gooey chickpea cookies (page 151)
+ Burgers and chippies (page 241)
+ Pink hummus (page 272) with veggies to dip
+ Apricot delights (page 147)
+ Beanie brownie bites (page 282).

ZINC

Zinc is an essential mineral required in the early years of life, but it doesn't stop there! Zinc is needed to support immune function, gut health, healthy growth, mood, behaviour, wound healing and cognitive development in growing children. Zinc has antioxidant properties along with supporting the body's inflammatory response.

Breastmilk and formula contain enough zinc to nutritionally support your baby until 6–7 months of age. After that, they need to get adequate zinc through wholefoods.

Zinc deficiency in children can lead to a compromised immune system, stunted growth, poor gut function, respiratory infections, suppressed appetite, slow cognition, slow recovery from illness and a lack of focus. The best way to avoid zinc deficiency is to offer a varied diet including foods rich in zinc.

FOODS RICH IN ZINC INCLUDE:

+ Beef
+ Lamb
+ Pork
+ Fish
+ Shellfish
+ Eggs
+ Peanuts
+ Chicken
+ Pepitas (pumpkin seed)
+ Plain yoghurt
+ Cashews
+ Chickpeas
+ White beans
+ Lentils
+ Cheese
+ Milk
+ Linseed (flax seed)
+ Wholegrains: quinoa, oats, corn, brown rice, barley, rye and spelt.

SIMPLE WAYS TO INCREASE YOUR LITTLE ONE'S ZINC INTAKE INCLUDE:

+ Grind up pumpkin seeds, cashews and almond and sprinkle on top of yoghurt or add to smoothies.
+ Mix ground linseed (flax seed) or almond meal into purées.
+ Coat spears of avocado or banana with almond meal.
+ Add ground linseed (flax seed) to a smoothie or porridge.
+ Choose wholegrains such as quinoa as opposed to refined grains such as white rice.
+ Replace wheat pasta with pulse pasta.

RECIPES RICH IN ZINC INCLUDE:

+ Meatballs and veggie sauce (page 144)
+ Burgers and chippies (page 241)
+ Slow-cooked lamb (page 237)
+ Sunshine loaf (page 306)
+ Thumbprint muffins (page 159)
+ Chewy cookies (page 289)
+ Nana zuke bread (page 135)
+ Nutty cookie dough balls (page 144)
+ Hearty lentil soup (page 225)
+ Veggie lentil curry (page 233)
+ Veggie-packed shepherd's pie (page 246)
+ Crunchy seed snaps (page 155)
+ Seed butter (page 267).

CALCIUM

Calcium is the most abundant mineral in the body. It's a key mineral, essential for healthy bones and teeth as well as supporting the development of a healthy nervous system. Adequate calcium consumption supports memory, learning and other crucial brain functions, which are significant for growing children.

Often people think dairy is the only way to get enough calcium, but while dairy is a wonderful source of calcium, there are many other great sources.

FOODS RICH IN CALCIUM* INCLUDE:

+ Cow's or goat's milk
+ Cow's yoghurt
+ Cheese
+ Sardines
+ Chia seeds
+ White beans
+ Almonds
+ Chickpeas
+ Tahini (unhulled)
+ Broccoli
+ Tinned salmon or sardines with bones
+ Nori
+ Spinach
+ Tofu
+ Lentils
+ Linseed (flax seed).

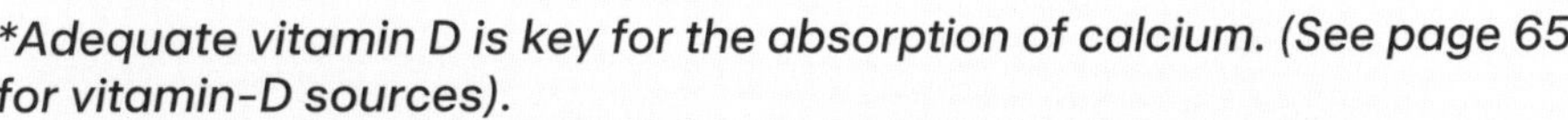
**Adequate vitamin D is key for the absorption of calcium. (See page 65 for vitamin-D sources).*

SIMPLE WAYS TO INCREASE YOUR LITTLE ONE'S CALCIUM INTAKE INCLUDE:

+ Mash sardines with avocado and hemp seeds and use as a spread on bread, or as a purée for younger babies.
+ Mix ground almonds, ground linseed (flax seed) and chia seeds into porridge.
+ Add ground almonds, ground linseed (flax seed) and chia seeds to a smoothie.
+ Put a scoop of our Berry good jam (page 275) on top of yoghurt.
+ Replace wheat pasta with legume-based pulse pasta.
+ Don't discard the bones in tinned salmon and sardines, crush them with your fingers and add to your little one's meals.
+ Offer nori as a snack.
+ Make frozen yoghurt ice blocks.
+ Switch up your regular flour for almond meal when baking.

RECIPES RICH IN CALCIUM INCLUDE:

+ Pink hummus (page 272) with veggies to dip or spread onto sandwiches
+ Berry yummy gummies (page 148)
+ Bable baked beans (page 106)
+ Super sardine bites (page 191)
+ Salmon bites (page 188)
+ Secret sauce (page 209)
+ Sushi (page 195)
+ Mac 'n' cheese (page 196)
+ Three-ingredient power balls (page 132).

IODINE

Iodine is an essential nutrient, which needs to be obtained through diet and is crucial for thyroid function. The thyroid gland produces hormones that control energy levels, metabolism, body temperature, heart rate, growth and development.

FOODS RICH IN IODINE INCLUDE:

+ Seaweed
+ Fish
+ Eggs
+ Dairy: milk, cheddar cheese, yoghurt, kefir and butter
+ Liver.

SIMPLE WAYS TO INCREASE YOUR LITTLE ONE'S IODINE INTAKE INCLUDE:

+ Offer seaweed as a snack.
+ Offer fresh fish a couple of times per week.
+ Include eggs on a regular basis.
+ Offer Greek yoghurt as a snack.
+ Cook with butter or douse veggies in it.
+ Add kefir to smoothies.

RECIPES RICH IN IODINE INCLUDE:

+ Sushi (page 195)
+ Super sardine bites (page 191)
+ Salmon bites (page 188)
+ Creamy coconut fish curry (page 226)
+ Green frittata (page 230)
+ Egg poppers (page 171)
+ Brekky-baked eggs (page 121)
+ Mac 'n' cheese (page 196)
+ The Med pasta (page 222)
+ Rainbow fish bake (page 245).

MAGNESIUM

Magnesium impacts your little one's quality of sleep and stress response, helps to regulate their mood and behaviour, supports their muscle and nerve function, regulates their blood sugar and supports energy levels. It's also crucial for bone development in the early years, making it an important nutrient to include in your baby's diet.

RICH SOURCES OF MAGNESIUM INCLUDE:

+ Almonds
+ Cashews
+ Spinach
+ Oats
+ Avocados
+ Edamame
+ Wholegrains: quinoa, oats, corn, brown rice and barley, rye or spelt
+ Kidney and black beans
+ Lentils
+ Bananas
+ Peanut butter
+ Pepitas (pumpkin seed)
+ Fish such as salmon, tuna and mackerel.
+ Chia seeds.

SIMPLE WAYS TO INCREASE YOUR LITTLE ONE'S MAGNESIUM INTAKE INCLUDE:

+ Replace wheat pasta with pulse pasta made from legumes.
+ Add nuts, ground pepita (pumpkin seed), nut butter, chia seeds or spinach to smoothies.
+ Use nut butter as a dip for veggie sticks or add nut butter to a sandwich.
+ Mix ground nuts, ground pepita (pumpkin seed), nut butter or Berry good jam (page 275) in porridge.
+ Spread nut butter on a banana.
+ Replace white flour in baking with almond flour.

RECIPES RICH IN MAGNESIUM INCLUDE:

+ Berry good jam (page 275)
+ Gooey chickpea cookies (page 151)
+ Blondie bites (page 285)
+ Berry yummy gummies (page 148)
+ Beanie brownie bites (page 282)
+ Chia pudding – three ways (page 117)
+ Nana zuke bread (page 135)
+ Turbo muffins (page 140)
+ Seed butter (page 267)
+ Veggie-packed shepherd's pie (page 246).

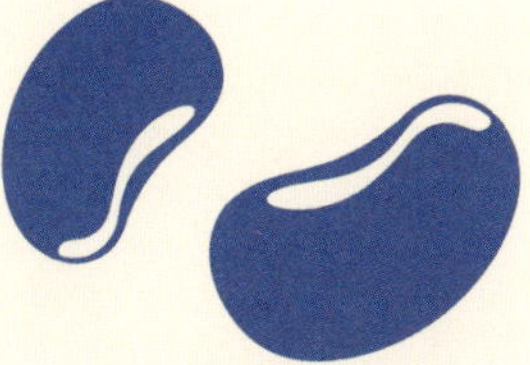

OMEGA-3 FATTY ACIDS/ DHA

Omega-3 fatty acids – also referred to as omega-3s – are an essential fatty acid, a critical nutrient for your little one's growth and development.

Omega-3s play a vital role in brain development and function, the nervous system, cognitive and neurological function and help to reduce and manage inflammation in the body, which is a primary driver of chronic disease. Omega-3s are shown to support children's learning, memory, mood, concentration and mental health.

FOODS RICH IN OMEGA-3S INCLUDE:

+ Salmon
+ Sardines
+ Mackerel
+ Tuna
+ Snapper
+ Grass-fed beef and lamb
+ Linseed (flax seed)/Linseed (flax seed) oil
+ Walnuts
+ Hemp seeds
+ Chia seeds
+ Green leafy veggies
+ Seaweed.

It's important to note animal-based omega-3s are more readily absorbed in the body as they come in the form of DHA, compared to sources from plant foods* that come in the form of ALA.

**Supplementation may be advised for babies on a plant-based diet. Speak to your healthcare provider for individual guidance.*

SIMPLE WAYS TO INCREASE YOUR LITTLE ONE'S OMEGA-3S INTAKE INCLUDE:

+ Add hemp seeds, ground linseed (flax seed)/LSA, walnuts, chia seeds or spinach to a smoothie.
+ Drizzle linseed (flax seed) oil onto veggies.
+ Mix chia seeds, hemp seeds, ground walnuts or ground linseed (flax seed) into porridge.
+ Offer seaweed as a snack.
+ Mix through our berry chia jam (page 275) into a bowl of yoghurt.
+ Buy grass-fed meat instead of grain-fed meat due to its higher omega-3s content.
+ Serve fish 1–2 times a week.

RECIPES RICH IN OMEGA-3S INCLUDE:

+ Super sardine bites (page 191)
+ Salmon bites (page 188)
+ Creamy coconut fish curry (page 226)
+ Slow-cooked lamb (page 237)
+ Sushi (page 195)
+ Berry yummy gummies (page 148)
+ Chia pudding – three ways (page 117)
+ Berry good jam (page 275).

CHOLINE

Choline is an essential nutrient for brain development in the early years. It impacts the health and function of the liver, metabolism and the nervous system. This impacts the way children learn and their memory. Consuming choline-rich foods is vital from pregnancy to babies, infants and beyond.

FOODS RICH IN CHOLINE INCLUDE:

+ Beef and chicken liver
+ Sardines
+ Mackerel
+ Eggs
+ Prawns (shrimp)
+ White fish
+ Beef
+ Lamb
+ Tinned salmon
+ Chicken breast
+ Brussels sprouts
+ Broccoli
+ Asparagus
+ Cauliflower
+ Peanuts/peanut butter
+ Almonds/almond butter.

SIMPLE WAYS TO INCREASE YOUR LITTLE ONE'S CHOLINE INTAKE INCLUDE:

+ Add a boiled egg to meals.
+ Add peanut or almond butter to a smoothie or porridge.
+ Grind up whole almonds and add them to porridge, a smoothie or yoghurt.
+ Sprinkle ground almonds on finger-sized pieces of banana or avocado.
+ Fry up brussels sprouts as a side with dinner.
+ Sprinkle liver powder into bolognese.

RECIPES RICH IN CHOLINE INCLUDE:

+ Custard oats (page 102)
+ Green frittata (page 230)
+ Egg poppers (page 171)
+ Speedy spinach omelette (page 110)
+ Chickpea pancrêpes (page 114)
+ Super sardine bites (Page 191)
+ Salmon bites (page 188)
+ Meatballs and veggie sauce (page 234)
+ Slow-cooked lamb (page 237)
+ Chicken soup (page 213)
+ Roast chook (page 06)
+ Chicken schnitty (page 214)
+ Rainbow fish bake (page 245).

VITAMIN A

Vitamin A contains antioxidants that help to protect your little one from chronic disease. Vitamin A is shown to support, develop and maintain a healthy immune system, helping the body fight off infections and further playing a key role in vision development and skin health.

FOODS RICH IN VITAMIN A* INCLUDE:

+ Liver
+ Tuna
+ Egg yolks
+ Cheddar cheese
+ Orange and yellow vegetables such as sweet potatoes, carrots and pumpkin (squash)
+ Leafy green vegetables such as kale, spinach and broccoli.

**Vitamin A is fat-soluble so make sure you pair these foods with a healthy fat to aid absorption (see page 70 for healthy fat sources).*

SIMPLE WAYS TO INCREASE YOUR LITTLE ONE'S VITAMIN A INTAKE INCLUDE:

+ Serve roasted sweet potatoes or pumpkin alongside a main meal.
+ Grate liver into bolognese or add liver powder.
+ Add leafy greens like spinach to a smoothie.
+ Try tinned fish in a sandwich or wrap.

RECIPES RICH IN VITAMIN A INCLUDE:

+ Monster pancakes (page 94)
+ Green frittata (page 230)
+ Egg poppers (page 171)
+ Cheesy broccoli bombs (page 200)
+ Speedy spinach omelette (page 110)
+ Salmon bites (page 188)
+ Custard oats (page 102)
+ Mac 'n' cheese (page 196)
+ Secret sauce (page 209)
+ The Med pasta (page 222).

VITAMIN B12

Vitamin B12 is one of the key ingredients in the production of DNA. It's crucial for the development of your child's growth, cognitive and neurological development, bone health, immune system and the formation of healthy red blood cells.

FOODS RICH IN VITAMIN B12* INCLUDE:

+ Beef liver
+ Beef
+ Salmon
+ Sardines
+ Tuna
+ Eggs
+ Milk
+ Yoghurt
+ Cheese.

**Supplementation may be advised for plant-based babies.*

SIMPLE WAYS TO INCREASE YOUR LITTLE ONE'S VITAMIN B12 INTAKE INCLUDE:

+ Stir in grated beef liver to bolognese or add liver powder.
+ Mash sardines with avocado and extra-virgin olive oil, add as a toast topper, in a sandwich or in a purée for babies.
+ Serve plain yoghurt pouches or mix yoghurt with fruit.
+ Regularly include eggs.

RECIPES RICH IN VITAMIN B12 INCLUDE:

+ Super sardine bites (page 191)
+ Salmon bites (page 188)
+ Meatballs and veggie sauce (page 234)
+ Mighty veggie bolognese (page 168)
+ Mac 'n' cheese (page 196)
+ Green frittata (page 230)
+ Egg poppers (page 171)
+ Custard oats (page 102)
+ Fluffy custard sticks (page 109).

VITAMIN C

One of the most renowned nutritional benefits of vitamin C is its function in supporting the immune system and fighting infection. However, that's not the only superpower of this incredible nutrient.

Vitamin C is also a powerful antioxidant: it helps protect our cells from damage by 'sweeping up' free radicals in the body. Vitamin C is also key for the absorption of other important minerals such as iron. It's a water-soluble vitamin so it's not able to be stored in the body. This means we need to replenish vitamin C sources daily to keep up with daily requirements.

FOODS RICH IN VITAMIN C INCLUDE:

+ Kiwi fruits
+ Broccoli
+ Spinach
+ Oranges
+ Berries
+ Red capsicum (bell pepper)
+ Papayas
+ Tomatoes
+ Cauliflower
+ Lemons
+ Mangoes
+ Brussels sprouts
+ Potatoes and sweet potatoes.

SIMPLE WAYS TO INCREASE YOUR LITTLE ONE'S VITAMIN C INTAKE INCLUDE:

+ Include fruits rich in vitamin C at snack and mealtimes, or serve a fruit salad as a side.
+ Make a potato and cauliflower mash.
+ Offer a plate of quartered cherry tomatoes and capsicum (bell pepper) sticks as a snack.
+ Add spinach or broccoli to a smoothie.
+ Squeeze lemon on fish or chicken.
+ Make potato and sweet potato chips.

RECIPES RICH IN VITAMIN C INCLUDE:

+ Supercharged squishies (page 172)
+ Cheesy broccoli bombs (page 200)
+ Green frittata (page 230)
+ Secret sauce (page 209)
+ Berry good jam (page 275)
+ Monster pancakes (page 94)
+ Berrylicious crumble (page 294)
+ Berry blast smoothie (page 167)
+ Mango ice blocks and jelly-tip ice blocks (page 297).

VITAMIN D

Vitamin D supports the development of healthy bones, muscles and teeth, and supports immune function.

A key role of vitamin D in the body is to help maintain and regulate calcium and phosphorus levels in the blood, an essential component of bone growth.

Unfortunately, vitamin D is not widely available from food as the main source is the sun and synthesising it into our skin.

FOODS RICH IN VITAMIN D INCLUDE:

+ Wild-caught salmon
+ Sardines
+ Beef and chicken livers
+ Egg yolk
+ Mushrooms.

SIMPLE WAYS TO INCREASE YOUR LITTLE ONE'S VITAMIN D INTAKE INCLUDE:

+ Place your mushrooms in the sun for 20 minutes (gill-side up) before cooking them.
+ Mix tinned salmon and sardines with avocado and use as a sandwich filler.
+ Add grated liver to bolognese.
+ Mix egg yolk through purées, when cooking.
+ Add mushrooms to bolognese or a stir fry.

RECIPES RICH IN VITAMIN D INCLUDE:

+ Custard oats (page 102)
+ Salmon bites (page 188)
+ Super sardine bites (page 191)
+ Green frittata (page 230)
+ Egg poppers (page 171).

TOP TIP

If you're concerned about your baby not consuming foods rich in any of the nutrients discussed in this chapter, please talk to your healthcare practitioner for advice around potential supplementation.

A BALANCED PLATE

Understanding what makes up a balanced plate is an incredibly valuable tool to support you when feeding your little one. A balanced plate is made up of macronutrients, which are the nutrients we need in large doses, including carbohydrates, protein and healthy fats, and micronutrients, which are the vitamins and minerals required in small doses.

Carbohydrates are the body's energy boosters, giving your little one the fuel they need to grow and play. Protein helps to build and strengthen little bodies. And let's not forget about the healthy fats! They play a vital role in keeping your little one satiated while also helping to regulate important hormones in the body.

Finding the right ratio of these macronutrients is what makes a balanced meal, keeping your little one's blood sugars stable and their tummy fuller for longer.

AIM FOR 1/4 OF THE PLATE TO BE SLOW-BURNING CARBOHYDRATES OR WHOLEGRAINS

+ Oats, quinoa, basmati or brown rice, barley, lentils, chickpeas, white beans, kidney beans, buckwheat, good-quality wholegrain breads, wholemeal pasta, wholegrain couscous, sweet potatoes and potatoes, pumpkin (squash), peas and corn.

AIM FOR 1/2 OF THE PLATE TO BE NON-STARCHY VEGGIES AND FRUIT

+ Veggies such as broccoli, cauliflower, cabbage, eggplant (aubergine), mushrooms, zucchini (courgette), green beans, tomatoes, cucumbers, asparagus, spinach, kale, capsicums (bell peppers), brussels sprouts, mushrooms and onion.
+ Fruit such as berries, kiwi fruit, melons, oranges, apples, pears, mangoes, grapes, apricots, peaches and plums.

AIM FOR 1/4 OF THE PLATE TO BE GOOD-QUALITY PROTEINS

+ Animal proteins such as red meat, chicken, turkey and eggs, white fish, wild salmon, sardines, mackerel, tuna, prawns (shrimp), cheese and yoghurt.
+ Plant-based sources such as tempeh, tofu, beans, edamame, chickpeas, nuts, nut butters, seeds and quinoa.

USE HEALTHY FATS IN MODERATION

+ Try to include avocado, cheese, nuts and nut butters, seeds (hemp seeds, chia seeds, linseed (flax seed), tahini), linseed (flax seed) oil, eggs, coconut oil, milk, ghee, grass-fed butter, extra-virgin olive oil, oily fish, hummus and yoghurt.

Aiming for a variety of these key nutrients will help broaden your little one's palate and, most importantly, will support a flourishing gut.

NON-STARCHY
FRUIT & VEG
PROTEIN
CARBOHYDRATES
HEALTHY FATS

CARBO-HYDRATES

Carbohydrates are a major component of your little one's diet. They feed their brain, fuel their metabolism and support the development of their immune, digestive and nervous systems. Most importantly, carbohydrates are the body's greatest source of energy.

Carbohydrates are often broken into two categories: quick- and slow-burning carbohydrates. The difference between them is the speed in which the carbohydrate enters the bloodstream and gives the body energy. The slower the carbohydrate enters the bloodstream, the more the blood sugars will remain balanced.

Quick, or refined, carbohydrates are stripped of key nutrients through the processing methods, making them 'empty carbohydrates'. Without fibre, they act as a fast energy source but fail to provide the same satiety as a slow carbohydrate, leading to unwanted energy spikes. Some examples of refined/quick carbs include white bread, white rice, wheat pasta and white flour.

BLOOD SUGAR

Blood sugar ('blood glucose') is the sugar found in the blood from the food we eat. It's the body's primary source of energy. When carbohydrates are consumed, the sugars in those foods are broken down into glucose and travel to the bloodstream to provide energy to the cells.

The rate in which the glucose 'sugar' reaches the bloodstream is extremely important, as the slower the transport, the less 'blood-sugar spike'. Once the cells absorb that glucose, the blood sugar falls or drops. Quick rises and falls create unstable blood-sugar levels. Over time, this is one of the primary risk factors of insulin-resistance leading to Type 2 diabetes.

'Slow carbohydrates/carbs' enter the bloodstream at a slower rate, slowing releasing the sugars 'glucose' into the body to then be absorbed and digested.

When carbohydrates contain vitamins, minerals and fibre, it slows down the transport time, taking longer to digest. This means the blood sugar rises slowly, in comparison to carbohydrates voided of these nutrients, travelling faster to the bloodstream and creating a spike in blood sugars.

A balanced meal supports and stabilises your little one's blood-sugar levels. This prevents spikes and dips, which make your little one's tummy rumble again shortly after eating. Instead, when their blood sugar is stable, they'll stay fuller for longer, feel alert, not have sudden hunger pangs and be able to concentrate on learning and having fun.

FRUIT

One of the biggest misconceptions about fruit is that it's high in sugar so you shouldn't eat too much of it. But as we know, not all sugar is created equal.

The difference between sugar in fruit and processed/refined sugars is that fruit contains naturally occuring sugars as well as an abundance of fibre, antioxidants and vitamins and minerals. In combination, these slow down the transit time of the sugar reaching the bloodstream. This means our kids won't get the 'sugar high' from fruit and the subsequent crash that foods with refined sugars give them.

Fruit is a wonderful source of vitamins and minerals and while it shouldn't be eaten in excess, it should absolutely be a part of a balanced diet. Aim to include two serves a day. As a bonus, because fruit is naturally sweet, it's a great alternative to processed sugary snacks.

So what about fruit juices?

While fruit juice can be part of a balanced diet, it's not the same as serving a whole fruit. When fruit is squeezed to make a juice, only the juice of that fruit is used. Unfortunately, the rest of the fruit that is discarded is where the dietary fibre lies. As we know, without that fibre, the transit into our bloodstream is much faster, spiking blood-sugar levels.

If you are going to offer juice, a better option is fruit juice mixed with vegetables to lower the overall sugar content of the juice.

PROTEIN

Protein is essential for the growth and development of every cell in the body. Protein is made up of amino acids (essential and non-essential), which are the body's building blocks.

Essential amino acids must be obtained through different dietary protein sources. This puts great emphasis on the need to offer a variety of protein-based foods, as all protein sources contain different amino acids, along with vitamins and minerals.

Protein is key to helping your little one stay full and balance blood-sugar levels so think of protein as an important part of every meal.

Our philosophy is that no one animal protein should be given in excess. Instead, have a balance throughout the week with other animal- and plant-based proteins. Aim for a variety of both animal and plant-based proteins throughout the day, such as different types of red meats, chicken, turkey, white fish, salmon, eggs, legumes, tofu, tempeh, nut butters and cheese.

FATS

Healthy fats support the body to make hormones, play a pivotal role in ensuring satiety after meals and are crucial for the absorption of the fat-soluble vitamins A, D, E and K. We need fat from early childhood to ensure healthy brain development and a variety of dietary fats is the key to reaping a range of nutritional benefits. However, it's important to note that not all fats are considered 'healthy fats'.

OILS

Each oil has differing compositions, heat stability and flavour. This all contributes to their purpose when cooking. Understanding their heat stability, or 'smoke point', is a significant factor when choosing what oil to cook with. While some oils can withstand high temperatures, others can be 'spoiled' when heated too high, breaking down and releasing harmful compounds and the development of free radicals, which can lead to cellular damage.

A diet rich in antioxidants helps to mop up free radicals in the body!

REFINED VS. UNREFINED OILS

Refined oils undergo significant heat and chemical solvents to extract the oil. Whereas unrefined oils are known as 'virgin' oils as the oil is extracted without heat or chemical solvents. When heat is applied the plants lose their nutritional properties, such as polyphenols, antioxidants and vitamins. Virgin or cold-pressed oils will keep nutrients intact and are the best options to look out for.

VEGETABLE AND SEED OILS

Vegetable or seed oils are made by extracting oil from the seeds using chemical solvents, bleach and are then deodorised, a highly refined process that strips all nutrients from their original sources. Due to their heavy processing methods, they are highly susceptible to oxidative damage. Vegetable oils are high in omega-6s. When we consume too many products containing these oils, our omega-6s to omega-3s ratio becomes imbalanced and can lead to inflammation in the body. Inflammation is the root cause of chronic disease.

TRANS FATS

Trans fats are created when oils and fats are hydrogenated or deodorised. Due to their known adverse effects on human health we want to aim to eliminate their consumption in our diet altogether. Trans fats increase the bad cholesterol in the body (LDL cholesterol) and reduce the good cholesterol (HDL cholesterol), which has been linked to the onset of heart disease and cognitive disorders. Trans fats are shown to cause inflammation in the body, which, as we discussed, can lead to the development of chronic disease. Trans fats are found in commercial baked goods, frozen goods, such as pizzas and spring rolls, margarines, fried foods, and packaged foods like sausage rolls and meat pies.

HEALTHY FATS AND HOW TO USE THEM

FAT	SMOKE POINT	USAGE	NUTRITIONAL NOTES
Avocado oil	270°C 520°F	Great for frying, baking and roasting, salad dressings and drizzling.	Rich in monounsaturated fats and antioxidants.
Ghee	250°C 480°F	Great for frying, baking and roasting.	Known as 'clarified butter', with the removal of the milk solids, ghee is an easier-to-digest option for little ones. Rich in vitamins and antioxidants.
Extra-virgin olive oil (EVOO)	207°C–210°C 400°F–410°F	Baking, roasting, marinades, light frying, sautéing, dressings and drizzling.	Rich in monounsaturated fats and antioxidants. EVOO is a better option than OO (olive oil) due to minimal processing.
Butter	175°C 347°F	Great for adding onto already cooked vegetables or baking.	A complex dietary fat rich in key vitamins such as A and D.
Cold-pressed coconut oil	175°C–204°C 347°F–400°F	Great for frying, sautéing, baking and roasting, especially with curries and baked goods.	High in saturated fats and antioxidants, and easily digested.
Linseed (flax seed) oil	107°C 225°F	Ideal for dressings, dips, adding to smoothies and drizzling onto foods to increase nutrient content.	Not for heating. A beautiful source of omega-3s.

FLOURISHING LITTLE GUTS

'SEVENTY PER CENT OF YOUR IMMUNE SYSTEM LIVES IN YOUR GUT, MAKING NUTRITION THE CORNERSTONE OF A THRIVING IMMUNE SYSTEM.'

Your baby's gut microbiome is an ecosystem made up of billions of bacteria that are responsible for supporting digestion; assisting with the absorption of key nutrients; supporting healthy bowels to remove waste; and supporting their immune system.

In fact, seventy per cent of your immune system lives in your gut, making nutrition the cornerstone of a thriving immune system. When there's imbalance in the ratio between good and bad bacteria, your little one's health can be compromised in the short and long term. To support the colonisation of good bacteria, and get rid of the bad bacteria, it's important to consume both prebiotic- and probiotic-rich foods.

PREBIOTICS

These non-digestible compounds are found in foods that help to feed healthy gut bacteria.

For example, garlic, onion, leek, mushrooms, seaweed, eggplant (aubergine), asparagus, apples, bananas, oats, chickpeas, lentils and kidney beans. By focusing on a diet rich in wholefoods like fruits, vegetables, legumes and wholegrains, this will increase the consumption of prebiotics.

PROBIOTICS

These are live cultures or 'microorganisms' that cultivate the balance of beneficial bacteria in the gut microbiome. They can be found in foods such as yoghurt, kefir, sauerkraut, tempeh, miso, sourdough and pickles.

Offering these foods is a great way to feed your little one's good bacteria. Probiotics can also be administered through supplementation*. However, we recommend food first and foremost as the best source of probiotics.

**If your little one doesn't consume these foods, we recommend consulting with a healthcare provider about a supplementation regime.*

FOODS THAT COMPROMISE OUR GUT HEALTH

Refined sugar and ultra-processed foods have been shown to compromise the integrity of the gut, and are a cause of inflammation in the body. Inflammatory conditions in little ones can present as eczema, asthma and allergies. This is another reason we recommend a wholefoods approach.

It's also important to understand the connection between the gut and the brain. Ninety per cent of the body's serotonin (the 'happy hormone') lives in the gut so a compromised gut can affect your little one's mood.

FIBRE

Fibre is found in fruits, vegetables and wholegrains and is critical for human health. Fibre is a crucial energy source that feeds the gut microbiome so it should be included in your little one's daily diet. When fibre is fermented by the gut it has a positive effect on the immune system. This is because it plays a role in feeding the good gut bugs, as well as health benefits to organs such as the kidneys, liver and brain.

A diet lacking in fibre contributes to conditions such as constipation, allergies, immune-related disorders and inflammatory conditions. The disruption it causes in the gut microbiome can increase the risk of developing diabetes later in life due to the impact it has on the regulation of blood-sugar levels. Fibre also plays a key role in the bulking of stools, your little one's bowel movements and their ability to excrete waste and toxins from the body.

TOP TIPS FOR INCREASING FIBRE INTAKE

+ Serve a diet rich in fruits and veggies. Variety is key! Make it a priority to introduce new fruits and veggies to your baby's plate often.
+ Add extra veggies to every meal: try our Mighty veggie bolognese (page 218) or our Secret sauce (page 209), which can be used on pasta or as a pizza sauce.
+ Swap refined carbohydrates for wholegrains: white bread to wholegrain/wholemeal bread, white rice to brown rice and regular couscous to wholemeal couscous.
+ Oats are a fibre-rich option. Try our Bable bircher (page 98), Everything oats (page 113) or Bouncy brekky bites (page 101).
+ Swap white pasta for wholegrain or pulse pastas.
+ Add nuts to your little one's diet via nut butters or grinding nuts down and sprinkling them on top of porridge or in a smoothie.
+ Serve dried fruit as a snack.
+ Chickpeas are full of fibre and are not just for savoury dishes: try our Three-ingredient power balls (page 132), Blondie bites (page 285) or Gooey chickpea cookies (page 151).
+ Add chia seeds to your little one's diet. Try our Chia pudding – three ways (page 117), Berry good jam (page 275) or Berry yummy gummies (page 148).

FOOD QUALITY

Quality matters, especially when feeding your family. How you nourish your baby can have a profound impact on their overall long-term health. From farm to plate, there is a lot that happens in between. Our goal is to empower you with the knowledge to make the healthiest choices you can for your family. Any change in the right direction is a positive change!

TOXIC LOAD

We live in a world full of thousands of different chemicals. These chemicals are found in the air we breathe, the water we drink and the food we eat. We often underestimate the importance of the early years when our children are growing, learning and developing at such a rapid rate.

As we are exposed to more and more of these everyday toxins, they start to accumulate in our body, adding to our 'toxic load'. These chemical toxins are shown to have an adverse effect on the developing brain, cognitive development, nervous system, behaviour, hormones and attention span. There is so much in our environment that we don't have control over so it's important we focus on what we can control.

HEAVY METALS

Heavy metals are derived from pollutants found in soil, which are shown to have a detrimental impact on human health. The main ones to pay close attention to are: arsenic, lead, mercury and cadmium. While the quantities found are small, the accumulation over time is what's worrisome. Unfortunately, emerging research shows the majority of packaged baby foods are found to have levels of heavy metals at doses undesirable for our little one's health, so we recommend not consuming them on a regular basis.

TOP TIPS FOR MINIMISING 'TOXIC LOAD' BUILD UP

+ Store food in glass jars or containers instead of plastic.
+ Buy BPA-free tinned and canned foods.
+ Wash non-organic fruit and veggies to help remove herbicides and pesticide residue (page 77).
+ Offer a diet rich in wholefoods and consume fewer packaged foods.
+ Use a water filter to reduce exposure to contaminated water supply.
+ Swap plastic bottles and lunchboxes with stainless steel ones.
+ Swap out plastic cutting boards for wooden ones.
+ Swap out rice food products (which are higher in arsenic) with other wholegrains.
+ Avoid regularly serving large fish with high-mercury content, such as shark (flake), swordfish, basa, perch, marlin, king mackerel, bluefin tuna. Instead, try sardines, salmon and mackerel or white fish such as snapper.

Any change you make today is helpful – change can be gradual but just remember, it all adds up!

THE DIRTY DOZEN™ AND THE CLEAN 15™

Pesticides are widely used in global agriculture. They are sprayed on crops to conserve their quality and, ultimately, to protect crops from pests. However, pesticides reduce the health benefits of fruits and vegetables, and have also been linked to having harmful impacts on human health. Unfortunately, children are more vulnerable to adverse health impacts due to their size, rapid growth and development, and their inability to detoxify compounds to the same degree as adults.

Each year, a US body called the Environmental Working Group (EWG) publishes a list of the most highly contaminated crops from pesticides and the least-contaminated crops. Although the lists are released annually, they don't change significantly from year to year. Foods with thicker skins are usually in the Clean 15™ as the pesticides are harder to penetrate through their skin. By comparison, the Dirty Dozen™ can have up to 23 different pesticides sprayed on each crop.

The Dirty Dozen™ and Clean 15™ are great indicators of what produce to prioritise purchasing organic if you can and when conventional produce is a-okay! This can reduce your and your little one's exposure to harmful chemicals by 80 per cent.

DIRTY DOZEN™ 2023*

1. Strawberries
2. Spinach
3. Kale/collard greens
4. Peaches
5. Pears
6. Nectarines
7. Apples
8. Grapes
9. Capsicum (bell pepper)
10. Cherries
11. Blueberries
12. Green beans

CLEAN 15™ 2023

1. Avocados
2. Sweet corn
3. Pineapple
4. Onions
5. Papaya
6. Peas
7. Asparagus
8. Honeydew melon
9. Kiwi fruit
10. Cabbage
11. Mushrooms
12. Mango
13. Sweet potatoes
14. Watermelon
15. Carrots

**The Dirty Dozen™ is based on where you live so we recommend checking online each year for the list that's most relevant to you.*

ALTERNATIVES TO BUYING ORGANIC

We understand that buying organic is not accessible to everyone. It can be extremely expensive and tricky to source so here are some ways to minimise your family's exposure to chemicals.

WASH YOUR VEGGIES!

Add 1 tablespoon of white vinegar or baking soda for every 2 cups of water. Soak produce for 12–15 minutes. This should remove most of the chemical residue. In addition, invest in a scrubbing brush and give them a little scrub after soaking, then rinse off. We do this all at once after a big shop rather than each time we're preparing food to save time and ensure our produce is ready to go.

BUY FROZEN!

When it comes to organic produce, try purchasing frozen organic varieties of foods such as berries, spinach, kale and green beans. Frozen vegetables are a much more affordable and nutritionally smart choice. Frozen vegetables are 'snap frozen' meaning they are frozen as they are picked so are at the height of their nutritional peak and ripeness. Sometimes this can lead to an even more nutritious choice as opposed to buying week-old veggies that lose some of their nutritional value each day they sit on the shelf.

TINNED VS. DRIED LEGUMES

TINNED LEGUMES

Tinned legumes, such as lentils, chickpeas and beans are a great, quick and easy option to have on hand in the pantry when you haven't done that grocery shop, or you have run out of time to cook an elaborate family meal.

It's important to look for BPA-free options, where possible. BPA stands for Bisphenol A, an industrial chemical found to be toxic to human health with high levels of exposure. BPA is found in the linings of some aluminium tins and leaches into food. BPA is categorised as an endocrine disruptor and has a negative impact on hormones, leading to adverse health effects over time.

Legumes can be hard to digest and soaking them helps this but tinned beans often aren't soaked before cooking. Soaking beans at home is one solution. Not only will it aid digestion, but it also improves the absorption of important vitamins and minerals in the legumes.

If you don't have the dried kind on hand, make sure to drain and rinse tinned varieties to reduce excess sodium.

DRIED LENTILS

Dried lentils are a great pantry staple. Not only are they incredibly affordable, but they soak up more flavour during the cooking process than the tinned kinds and you don't have to worry about BPA.

It's important to note that dried lentils take much longer to prepare and cook.

SOAKING SIMPLIFIED

Soaking grains and legumes before eating them is highly beneficial for their nutritional value. It helps break down starches, improve absorption, and aid digestion. Grains and legumes naturally contain compounds like phytic acid, which can be hard for our bodies to break down and digest and especially hard for your little one's maturing digestive system! These compounds can stop the body from absorbing important minerals like iron, calcium and zinc. Soaking with an acidic compound such as lemon or apple-cider vinegar helps to remove the phytase, allowing our bodies to better utilise the nutrients from food.

HOW TO SOAK GRAINS/LEGUMES

1. Place the grains/legumes in a spacious container, keeping in mind that they will expand in size.
2. Cover with cool water, leaving a few centimetres of extra water on top. Add a squeeze of lemon or a dash of apple-cider vinegar.
3. Let the grains/legumes soak for 8–10 hours at room temperature, or if the weather is hot, you can refrigerate them. Drain the grains/legumes before cooking.

COMPARING FARMING PRACTICES

Quality matters when consuming animal-based foods on a regular basis and it's important to understand that not all animal produce go through the same farm-to-table process.

MEAT AND POULTRY

OUR CHOICE:

+ **Pasture-raised:** Animals are free to roam in their natural environment for the majority of their lives.
+ **Grass-fed:** Animals are fed grass instead of grains, with no GMO ingredients. Grass-fed animals are also richer in nutrients such as vitamin A and E and have a healthier ratio of omega-3s to omega-6s.
+ **Organic:** Their feed is free of herbicides, pesticides, GMOs and the animals are not given growth hormones or antibiotics.
+ **Free-range:** The term 'free-range' refers to a method of farming whereby animals spend a portion of their day roaming freely outdoors with sunshine and fresh air, in comparison to being confined in cages with zero roaming. In some cases, these animals are given antibiotics* if necessary and GMO feeds. Look for 'antibiotic-free' and 'GMO-free' when purchasing free-range products.

ENJOY IN MODERATION:

+ **Grain-fed:** These animals eat a diet of grains, synthetic feeds and GMO feeds that can be exposed to pesticides and other chemicals.
+ **Caged:** Eggs from chickens that spend their life in cages. They aren't allowed to roam freely and this subsequently increases their stress levels.

**The issue with animals having antibiotics is that it contributes to the global problem of 'antibiotic resistance', meaning when we need antibiotics to actually fight illness, our body is resistant to it through overexposure through the food we are eating.*

FISH

OUR CHOICE:

+ **Wild-caught fish:** Fish caught straight from the ocean, rivers or lakes, i.e. from the natural habitat in which they live. Wild-caught fish live off smaller fish and algae, so they are full of omega-3s.

ENJOY IN MODERATION:

+ **Farmed fish:** Farmed fish are raised in tanks. Due to overcrowding, disease and bacteria breed, so antibiotics and pesticides often need to be used which then accumulates in the fish we consume. Farmed fish may eat GMO corn and soy, palm oil and heavily processed grains not to mention the associated contaminants and heavy metals. They are likely to contain fewer omega-3s as their diet is not primarily other fish like in the wild. Farmed salmon is given its rich pink colour from the use of synthetic colour dyes.

DAIRY

OUR CHOICE:

+ **Yoghurt:** Look for full-fat, whole-milk natural yoghurt without additives. We also like goat's milk, sheep's milk, kefir or Greek yoghurt.
+ **Milk:** Choose organic, full-fat milk from grass-fed cows, where possible. Avoid buying skim milk or low-fat milk for your little one.
+ **Cheese:** Look for cheeses without any additives. If you need grated cheese, grate it yourself rather than buying pre-shredded cheese as grated cheese usually contains additives.

ENJOY IN MODERATION:

+ **Flavoured yoghurt pouches:** These are often filled with sugar and additives, so we try to limit to a sometimes food.

PLANT-BASED MILKS

As we have discussed earlier, if your baby is formula fed, there is no nutritional need for cow's milk after weaning off formula at 12 months.

While plant-based milks can be fortified with calcium, we recommend offering your little one calcium from natural sources as it's more easily absorbed. If you feel like your baby is not consuming enough wholefoods rich in calcium then incorporating plant-based milks into their diet can be beneficial.

Check the ingredients list for any additives, preservatives and sweeteners. Instead look for plant-based milks with a simple, minimal and recognisable ingredients list, always aim for unsweetened (without added sugars) and choose one without vegetable oils. Canned coconut milk, with just coconut extract and water, can be a great alternative to the plant milks you'll find in the supermarket if your little one is getting ample calcium from wholefood sources.

GMOS

GMOs (genetically modified organisms) are a widespread global farming practice whereby the DNA of plants, animals and microorganisms have been genetically altered in a laboratory.

While advantageous to farmers to help maintain crop supply, consuming GMO foods has been shown to cause major problems in human health, with children more vulnerable to the impact of GMOs due to their rapidly growing bodies and immature digestive systems. Yet over 80 per cent of supermarket products contain GMO ingredients!

The main foods containing GMOs are soy and corn, (hello, vegetable oils!), wheat products and milk. Look for GMO-free options and, where possible, choose organic as organic means they will not contain GMOs.

DECODING ADDITIVES

Packaged foods can be heavily processed, with key nutrients stripped out through the process and replaced with additives and preservatives to enhance flavour, texture and preserve shelf life. Essentially the end product is often far removed from the 'food' it began as.

Children are more vulnerable to the impact of additives due to their developing systems. Additives can alter gut health, behaviour, lead to or heighten the onset of allergies and eczema, mood and sleep, and lead to hyperactivity. It's important to be aware of additives like colourings, nitrates, sulphites, thickeners, emulsifiers, anti-caking agents, food acids, vegetable gums, stabilisers, MSG, aspartame, natural and artificial flavours, to name a few. Even 'natural flavours' can be misleading as manufacturers use this as an umbrella term, without any legal need for disclosure. In fact, a 'natural flavour' can contain up to a hundred different chemically derived ingredients.

So what can you do? Limit packaged foods and focus on predominately 'real food' – wholefoods in their natural state.

TOP TIPS FOR READING NUTRITION LABELS

+ The first ingredient in the ingredient list is the most abundant in that product. Be mindful if you see a form of sugar listed as one of the top ingredients.
+ Ensure the ingredients are recognisable to you. Be cautious of preservatives and additives.
+ The per 100 g (3½ oz) column in the nutrition panel is the best form of comparison from product to product.
    + A low-sugar option is 5 g (⅛ oz)/100 g (3½ oz) or LESS, aim for no more than 10 g (¼ oz)/100 g (3½ oz)
    + A high-fibre option is 5 g (⅛ oz)/100 g (3½ oz) or MORE
    + A low-sodium option is 120 mg (4½ oz)/100 g (3½ oz) or LESS

TOP TIPS FOR RAISING INTUITIVE EATERS

If the fussy eating phase catches you by surprise (or is a particularly long one), here are our top tips for making things easier and getting your little one enjoying more variety and nutrients.

1. Keep offering a wide variety of flavours, colours and textures.
2. Don't overcrowd their plate. Keep servings small so you don't overwhelm your child. You can always offer more if they finish their plate.
3. Always include a 'safe food' – something you know they usually enjoy, especially if you're offering a meal your little one is unfamiliar with.
4. Change the environment of the meal. For example, have a picnic-style dinner or try a booster seat at the adults' table instead of a highchair.
5. Don't pressure your child to eat. Avoid saying 'Just taste it, you might like it!' or 'Just one more bite'. When children feel pressured to eat, it can lead to anxiety, resistance and create a negative association with mealtime.
6. Eat the same meal. As they say: 'Monkey see, monkey do'. Your little one is more likely to eat a meal if they see you eating it too. This might even mean letting them eat off your plate.
7. Eat together as a family as much as possible. This is not only beneficial for modelling how to eat, but sets up solid foundations for connection and forming positive eating habits.
8. Let your child make a mess! Don't worry, it does eventually get easier so embrace this beneficial time of exploration.
9. Avoid using food as a reward or to bribe your little one. This can contribute to developing an emotional crutch for 'treat foods' and disliking non-reward foods.
10. Don't label foods as 'good' or 'bad' – rather treat all foods equally. By restricting certain foods and telling your little ones they are 'bad', they're more likely to crave them.
11. Get your child involved in food prep and helping in the kitchen. This is a great way to expose them to food, even if they don't actually eat it. Just interacting with food is beneficial for exposure.
12. The goal isn't to finish everything on their plate. Let them listen to their body and trust their appetite. This will support their journey to becoming an intuitive eater.
13. Avoid offering alternatives once you have served a meal. If they ask for an alternative, use a standard phrase such as 'This is what's on the menu tonight, but we can have X tomorrow'. Stay firm and eventually they should start eating the meal you prepared.

14. Don't give up if your child has rejected food a few times. It can take up to fifteen exposures before they come around to that food.
15. Make the environment fun – play music, sing songs, keep mealtimes as positive and enjoyable as possible so they are a time to look forward to.
16. Offer buffet-style meals so your little one can choose what to put on their plate. This is another great way to expose them to new foods as well as let them exert their independence.
17. Give your child space. Try not to let them see your anxiety or frustration if they are not eating their meal. A happy and relaxed mealtime can help your child feel confident and willing to try new foods.
18. Avoid snacks too close to mealtime. This will help them to build up an appetite and they may be more likely to try their meal as opposed to filling up on snacks.
19. Avoid 'hiding' vegetables. While we encourage you to pack as much goodness into meals, it's best to be open about what's in the meal to avoid any distrust. You can even have your little one help to prepare the meal to see what's going in it. Alongside meals with veggies that aren't as obvious, ensure you are also still offering some they can see, touch and interact with.
20. Jazz up your veggies! Offering a dip or some grated cheese or butter on them not only adds some delicious flavour but makes eating veggies fun.

RECIPES

NOTES

COOKING EQUIPMENT

The recipes in this book require a few key basic pieces of equipment.

MUFFIN TIN

Use a 12-hole muffin tin, unless otherwise specified. Grease the tin with your oil of choice unless you're using silicone muffin moulds.

LOAF TIN

Our loaf recipes were made using a standard 24 × 14 × 7 cm (9½ × 5½ × 7¾ in) loaf tin. You can definitely use a smaller tin if that's all you have on hand, but keep an eye on the oven as cooking times may vary. We also recommend lining your tin with baking paper unless you're using a silicone mould.

PANS

Use a medium frying pan, unless otherwise specified. When cooking pancakes or fritters, a non-stick pan works best.

SAUCEPANS

Use a medium saucepan, unless otherwise specified.

CUPS + SPOONS

CUPS

This book uses metric cup measurements, i.e. 250 ml for 1 cup; in the US a cup is 8 fl oz, just smaller, and American cooks should be generous in their cup measurements; in the UK a cup is 10 fl oz and British cooks should be scant with their cup measurements.

TABLESPOONS

This book uses 15 ml (½ fl oz) tablespoons; cooks with 20 ml (¾ fl oz) tablespoons should be scant with their tablespoon measurements.

OVEN SETTINGS

The recipes in this book were cooked in a fan-forced (convection) oven. If using a conventional oven, increase the temperature by 20°C (70°F).

KEY

Each recipe has a key indicating if this recipe is suited to you and your little one.

SERVES

This indicates the number of adult servings. We have used adult portions as a guide because each child's appetite can vary significantly, and younger babies may only want smaller portions.

PREP TIME

The estimated amount of time it will take to gather and prepare all the necessary ingredients before starting the actual cooking process. It includes tasks like chopping vegetables, measuring ingredients and any other pre-cooking preparations.

COOK TIME

The estimated time for cooking the dish. It's important to note that cooking times may vary depending on factors such as the size of the portions or the specific heat source being used, i.e. induction vs. gas stovetop.

COOL TIME

The estimated amount of time required for a recipe to set to a desired consistency before it is ready to be served. During the cool time, we recommend leaving the dish undisturbed in the freezer or fridge to facilitate the setting process, even though it may be tempting to tuck in early!

AGE

We have given each recipe an age recommendation, from suitable for 6 months through to 24 months and beyond!

ALLERGEN

If a recipe contains one or more of the Top 9 allergens – eggs, peanuts, tree nuts, sesame, fish, shellfish, soy, dairy and wheat – you'll see the symbols below.

VEGAN

These recipes contain no animal products or by-products.

VEGETARIAN

May contain dairy and/or eggs but no other animal products.

5 INGREDIENTS OR LESS

Less is more! You can count the ingredients in these recipes on one hand.

20 MINUTES OR LESS

Life can be fast-paced and chaotic. These are quick recipes that can be prepped and cooked in 20 minutes or less.

NIGHT BEFORE

These recipes require a little advance planning with a step or two the night before.

LUNCHBOX FRIENDLY

These recipes play by the rules. Firstly, to keep things safe, we ditch the peanuts and tree nuts. These foods pose the highest risk among food allergies and are more likely to result in serious allergic reactions. These recipes mostly hold up well in a lunchbox for a few hours or may require an insulated lunchbox or cooler pack. Some schools have custom regulations around lunchboxes, so always double check with your educator before including any allergens.

FREEZER FRIENDLY

Indicates that the recipes can be frozen, giving you the superpower of conquering the chaos on busy days. See storage instructions at the bottom of the recipe.

TO SERVE

Serving suggestions to balance out a dish or to take it to new levels.

SWAPSIES

Indicates a recipe can be adapted for vegans, vegetarians, or has a suitable allergen swap. We also include ingredient swaps in case you're caught short.

STORAGE

This section indicates whether the recipe is best enjoyed immediately, or if it can be stored in the fridge, freezer or pantry for later. It provides information on how to store the recipe and for how long so you can enjoy every bite at the perfect time.

FIRST FOOD

This indicates if the recipe can be enjoyed as a first food. These recipes do not contain any allergens and can be prepared in a safe way for baby to enjoy as a very first food, be it as a purée or a finger food.

BREAKFAST

AGE
6 months +

SERVES
Makes 20 mini pancakes

PREP TIME
5 minutes

COOK TIME
20 minutes

MONSTER PANCAKES

- 1 large ripe banana, peeled and roughly chopped
- 1 cup fresh or frozen spinach
- ¾ cup rolled oats
- 2 eggs
- ¼ cup tinned coconut milk
- 1 teaspoon ground cinnamon
- 1 tablespoon coconut oil

TO SERVE

Top with your yoghurt of choice, our Berry good jam (page 275), nut butter and sprinkle with hemp seeds.

Your little one is sure to love these nutritious and fun pancakes! They're great for breakfast and also make the perfect snack. With the addition of spinach, you get an extra serve of greens in and a hit of iron (along with the oats). Pair the pancakes with a food rich in vitamin C like our Berry good jam or kiwi fruit to increase the absorption of the iron.

Blitz the banana, spinach, oats, eggs, coconut milk and cinnamon in a blender until a smooth batter forms.

Melt the coconut oil in a frying pan over a medium heat. Smear the pan with paper towel to help evenly distribute the oil.

Once the oil has melted, pour 1 tablespoon amounts of the pancake batter evenly into the pan to make mini pancakes.

Flip over when the pancakes start to bubble and no longer look 'gooey'. This will take about 2–3 minutes.

Repeat until all the batter is used up.

Transfer to a plate but don't be surprised if they don't all make it to the table!

SWAPSIES

For an egg-free version, swap eggs for flax eggs (page 50).

For a gluten-free version, swap oats 1:1 for buckwheat flour.

Swap coconut milk for any other milk of choice.

STORAGE

Store in an airtight container in the fridge for up to 5 days or in the freezer for up to 3 months. If freezing, use sheets of baking paper in between each pancake to avoid them sticking.

SERVES
Makes 30 mini pancakes

PREP TIME
5 minutes

COOK TIME
20 minutes

AGE
6 months +

HEARTBEET PANCAKES

These delicious pink pancakes are a fun way to add beetroot into your little one's diet. This recipe makes a large batch so there are always leftovers for the freezer! The hero ingredient beetroot (beet) is a powerful antioxidant, meaning it sweeps up free radicals in the body and has anti-inflammatory properties. Rich in fibre, beetroot supports digestion and bowel movement and is rich in nutrients like vitamin C, folate, potassium and magnesium. These pink pancakes will be loved by all!

250 g (9 oz) pre-cooked beetroot (beet), peeled

¾ cup rolled oats

1 large banana, peeled and roughly chopped

2 eggs

¼ cup yoghurt of choice

1 tablespoon coconut oil

Blitz the beetroot, oats, banana, eggs and yoghurt in a blender until smooth.

Melt the coconut oil in a frying pan over a low heat. Smear with paper towel to help evenly distribute the oil.

Once the pan is hot, make heart-shaped pancakes by using 2 teaspoons of batter to form a heart or 1 tablespoon for round mini pancakes.

Flip the pancakes when the batter starts to bubble and no longer looks 'gooey' – this will take about 3–4 minutes.

This recipe makes more than enough pancakes for one meal with extras for the freezer!

TO SERVE

Top with your yoghurt of choice, our Berry good jam (page 275), nut butter and sprinkle with hemp seeds.

SWAPSIES

For an egg-free version, swap eggs for flax eggs (page 50).

For a gluten-free version, swap oats 1:1 for buckwheat flour.

STORAGE

Store in the fridge for up to 5 days in an airtight container or in the freezer for up to 3 months. If freezing, use sheets of baking paper in between each pancake to avoid them sticking.

AGE
6 months +

SERVES
2

PREP TIME
5 minutes

COOL TIME
Overnight (or for a minimum of 3 hours)

BABLE BIRCHER

- 1 cup rolled oats
- 1 tablespoon ground linseed (flax seed)
- 1 grated apple (remove the skin for younger babies or purée)
- 1 tablespoon chia seeds
- 1 tablespoon hemp seeds
- ½ teaspoon ground cinnamon
- ¾ cup yoghurt of choice
- ½ cup water or milk of choice
- 1 teaspoon vanilla extract
- Squeeze of lemon juice

TO SERVE

Top with your favourite fruits or our Berry good jam (page 275) and nut butter.

This bircher muesli is great for mornings when you're short on time or your little one is just too hungry to wait for breakfast to be ready. It needs to be prepared the night before but don't worry, your morning self will thank you. It's a perfectly balanced breakfast rich in healthy fats, omega-3s, wholegrains and protein.

Mix all the ingredients together in a large bowl.

Add the mixture to an airtight container and store in the fridge overnight (or for a minimum of 3 hours).

STORAGE

Store in the fridge for up to 5 days in an airtight container.

SERVES
3

PREP TIME
10 minutes

COOL TIME
3 hours

AGE
6 months +

BOUNCY BREKKY BITES

These are one of our favourite food-prep items. They only take 10 minutes to whip up and make enough for a few brekkies. We love to switch up the fillings and you can add just about anything. They're bound by gelatin, which adds protein to your little one's morning oats and is also great for gut health.

FOR THE BASE

1½ cups rolled oats

1 cup milk of choice

1 cup filtered water or bone broth

MIX AND MATCH EXTRAS

½ chopped banana

½ grated apple

¼ cup frozen berries

1 teaspoon ground cinnamon

1 tablespoon hemp seeds

1 tablespoon ground linseed (flax seed)

3 serves liver powder (stirred in once the mixture is off the heat)

1 teaspoon honey*

**Omit honey for babies under 12 months.*

FOR THE GELATIN

3 tablespoons grass-fed gelatin

120 ml (4 fl oz) filtered water

Add the base ingredients to a saucepan over a low heat and stir until all the liquid is absorbed by the oats.

Stir in your extras of choice.

In a small mixing bowl, bloom your gelatin by stirring the gelatin and water together until the mixture becomes fluffy. This takes roughly 30 seconds.

Pour the mixture into the saucepan with the base ingredients and stir until the gelatin mixture has completely melted.

Pour into a medium-sized glass container with a flat bottom or silicone moulds and leave to set in the fridge for at least 3 hours (or ideally overnight).

Cut into age-appropriate, finger-shaped pieces or into bite-sized pieces for babies over 9 months.

SWAPSIES

For a softer texture, reduce gelatin to 2 tablespoons and water to 80 ml (2½ fl oz).

If you'd like to soak the oats the night before see our instructions on page 79.

STORAGE

Store in the fridge for up to 5 days in an airtight container.

TO SERVE

Top with your yoghurt of choice and our Berry good jam (page 275).

AGE
6 months +

SERVES
2

PREP TIME
2 minutes

COOK TIME
10 minutes

CUSTARD OATS

- 1 cup rolled oats
- 1 cup water
- 1 cup milk of choice
- 1 large banana, peeled and mashed
- ¼ teaspoon ground cinnamon
- 1 egg

TO SERVE

Top with poached pears, some more cinnamon and your yoghurt of choice or our Berry good jam (page 275), nut butter and hemp seeds.

We love this breakfast hack as the egg boosts the protein content of your standard bowl of oats. Eggs also have lots of beautiful nutrients like iron, choline, B12 and vitamin D. The finished porridge is creamy and delicious – so don't be surprised if your little one asks for seconds!

Cook the oats, water and milk in a saucepan over a low–medium heat.

Stir well for 5 minutes until the oats are a creamy consistency and all the liquid has been absorbed.

Stir in the mashed banana and cinnamon.

Once the porridge is almost ready, add in the egg and stir for a minute or so until the egg is cooked through and the porridge is creamy.

SWAPSIES

If you'd like to soak the oats the night before see our instructions on page 79.

STORAGE

These oats are best enjoyed warm but can be stored in the fridge for up to 2 days or in the freezer for up to 2 months. If frozen, make sure to thaw before reheating.

SERVES
Makes 6 crêpes

PREP TIME
5 minutes

COOK TIME
20 minutes

AGE
6 months +

EASY-PEASY CRÊPES

Our chickpea crêpes are high in protein and iron, and can be served sweet or savoury. They're great for breakfast, lunch or as a quick snack. You can experiment with various fillings to create your own unique flavour combinations. We love classic PB&J crêpes or filling them with cheese and spinach.

FOR THE CRÊPE BASE

- 1 cup besan (chickpea flour)
- 1¼ cups water (or milk of choice)
- ½ teaspoon ground cinnamon
- 1 tablespoon coconut oil

Blitz the base ingredients in a blender until smooth.

Melt coconut oil in a frying pan over a medium heat. Smear with paper towel to help evenly distribute the oil.

Pour in ¼ cup of batter, tilt the pan and work in a circular motion to ensure the batter is spread thinly and evenly.

Once you notice the edges starting to curl, your crêpe is ready to flip. Allow 1–2 minutes to cook on the other side.

FOR THE PB&J FILLING

Once your crêpe is cooked and transferred to a plate, spread on some nut butter of choice and a dollop of our Berry good jam (page 275).

Roll the crêpe up and trim the ends to create the perfect roll.

FOR THE CHEESE AND SPINACH FILLING

Once you've flipped the crêpe, add a handful of grated cheddar cheese, a good handful of spinach, a dash of paprika and freshly ground black pepper and cook until the cheese melts.

Roll the crêpe up and trim the ends to create the perfect roll.

STORAGE

Separate crêpes with baking paper to avoid sticking. Store in the fridge for up to 3 days in an airtight container.

To reheat, either microwave or warm the crêpes in a frying pan for 30 seconds.

AGE
6 months +

SERVES
4–6

PREP TIME
10 minutes

COOK TIME
15 minutes

BABLE BAKED BEANS

- 2 tablespoons extra-virgin olive oil
- 2 garlic cloves, roughly chopped
- 1 brown onion, diced
- 1 capsicum (bell pepper), finely chopped
- 1 zucchini (courgette), finely grated and drained
- 2 teaspoons dried basil
- 2 tablespoons tomato paste (concentrated purée)
- ½ cup vegetable stock
- 800 g (28 oz) tinned cannellini beans, drained and rinsed

TO SERVE

Serve with toast and a side of eggs and avocado. You can also top the beans with grated cheese or hemp seeds.

FIRST FOOD

Blitz the beans into a purée and add bone broth (page 279) or breastmilk/formula to thin.

Our baked beans are a family favourite. Packed with protein and veggies, they are great as a meal on their own or as a side dish. Cannellini beans are an excellent source of fibre, folate, iron and magnesium. The capsicum (bell pepper) and zucchini (courgette) up the ante on the everyday tomato-based baked beans.

Heat the extra-virgin olive oil in a large frying pan over a medium heat.

Add the garlic and onion and sauté for a couple of minutes.

Add the capsicum, zucchini and dried basil and cook for a further 5 minutes or until the capsicum and zucchini are tender. Set your pan aside.

Add the cooked ingredients to a food processor with the tomato paste and stock and blitz until very smooth.

Reheat your reserved frying pan over a low–medium heat. Pour in your sauce then add your canned beans. Cook the beans until warmed through. Season, if desired.

SWAPSIES

You can use 1½ cups dried cannellini beans in place of 800 g (28 oz) tinned cannellini beans. To prepare dried beans, soak them overnight according to instructions on page 79.

STORAGE

Store in the fridge for up to 5 days or in the freezer for up to 5 months.

SERVES
4

PREP TIME
5 minutes

COOK TIME
10 minutes

AGE
8 months +

   5 

FLUFFY CUSTARD STICKS

French toast has become a tradition in our households on the weekend: it's quick and easy and a brekky everyone enjoys. Eggs are a great source of protein and healthy fats while also containing essential vitamins and minerals. French toast is a clever way to offer eggs if your little one doesn't usually like the texture or taste. We love to use sourdough as it's fermented so great for everyone's gut health!

2 eggs

1 teaspoon ground cinnamon

4 pieces sourdough

1 tablespoon coconut oil

2 bananas, peeled and sliced lengthways

Whisk the eggs and cinnamon together in a large bowl.

Heat a large frying pan over a low heat.

Melt the coconut oil and wipe any excess oil off with a paper towel.

Dip the bread into the egg mixture and let it soak for 1 minute on each side.

Add your soaked bread to the pan. Cook for 2–3 minutes on each side until golden.

Add the banana halves alongside the bread and lightly pan-fry until golden on both sides.

Cut the toast into age-appropriate pieces and serve with the banana on top or mash the banana onto the toast for ease of eating.

TO SERVE

Add a tablespoon of smooth peanut butter or nut butter of choice, our Berry good jam (page 275) and your yoghurt of choice either dolloped on top or served in a bowl for dipping the toast fingers in.

STORAGE

Best enjoyed warm out of the frying pan.

AGE
6 months +

SERVES
1

PREP TIME
2 minutes

COOK TIME
2 minutes

SPEEDY SPINACH OMELETTE

- 1 teaspoon extra-virgin olive oil
- ¼ cup fresh or frozen spinach
- 2 eggs
- 2 teaspoons hemp seeds

TO SERVE

Serve with toast and add some healthy fat like slices of avocado.

Elevate your little one's breakfast with our omelette. With just a few simple ingredients, this dish is a wholesome start to the day. Eggs are a rich source of high-quality protein and they contain important vitamins and minerals like vitamin B12 and choline. The addition of spinach adds some vibrant colour, is a serving of greens on their plate and contains nutrients such as vitamin C and iron. Hemp seeds also add an extra protein hit and a healthy dose of omega-3s.

Heat the extra-virgin olive oil in a small frying pan over a medium heat.

Add the spinach and sauté for 1 minute or until it starts to wilt.

Whisk together the eggs and hemp seeds in a small bowl.

Pour the egg mixture on top of the spinach and let it cook until the egg is no longer runny. This should take approximately 2–4 minutes. Fold the omelette in half and let it cook through for another minute.

SWAPSIES

Swap the spinach for frozen peas.

STORAGE

Cut the omelette into strips and enjoy warm out of the frying pan.

SERVES
2

PREP TIME
2 minutes

COOK TIME
10 minutes

AGE
6 months +

EVERYTHING OATS

This porridge is the ultimate way to load up your oats with goodness. Start the day off right with a boost of omega-3s, fibre, protein and antioxidants. Add some nut butter or your yoghurt of choice and you're ready to go. Make these oats the night before so you're prepped for a few days, which is especially helpful if your little one is an early bird.

FOR THE BASE

1 cup rolled oats

1 cup milk of choice

1 cup filtered water or Bone broth (page 279)

OUR FAVOURITE EXTRAS

1 zucchini (courgette), finely grated and drained

½ chopped or mashed banana

1 teaspoon ground cinnamon

1 tablespoon hemp seeds

1 tablespoon LSA or ground linseed (flax seed)

Small handful of finely chopped fresh or frozen spinach

1 tablespoon grass-fed collagen

Add your base ingredients to a saucepan set over a medium heat. Stir well until all the liquids have soaked into the oats and there's a creamy consistency. This should take approximately 5 minutes.

Add your extras and stir well. Cook for another minute or so. If adding frozen ingredients, ensure they melt into the porridge before serving.

TO SERVE

Top with Berry good jam (page 275), your favourite fruits, chia seeds or hemp seeds, nut or seed butter, and a dollop of your yoghurt of choice.

SWAPSIES

If you'd like to soak the oats the night before see our instructions on page 79.

STORAGE

Best enjoyed warm out of the saucepan but can be stored in the fridge for up to 2 days.

AGE
6 months +

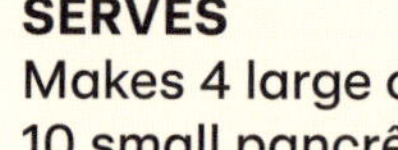

SERVES
Makes 4 large or 10 small pancrêpes

PREP TIME
5 minutes

COOK TIME
10 minutes

CHICKPEA PANCRÊPES

- 1 large overripe banana, peeled and roughly chopped
- ⅓ cup besan (chickpea flour)
- 3 eggs
- ¼ teaspoon ground cinnamon
- 1 tablespoon coconut oil

TO SERVE

Fill with Berry good jam (page 275), smooth peanut butter and your yoghurt of choice.

These fluffy pancrêpes are an incredibly delicious and nutrient-rich breakfast. Besan (chickpea flour) is a high-protein flour alternative, which is packed with the nutritional benefits of legumes and will ensure everyone starts their day with a full tummy.

Blitz all the ingredients, except the coconut oil, in a blender until smooth.

Melt the coconut oil in a frying pan over a medium heat. Smear with paper towel to help evenly distribute the oil.

Pour ¼ cup of batter into the hot frying pan, tilt the pan and work in a circular motion to ensure the batter is spread thinly and evenly.

Cook for 2–3 minutes, running a spatula along the edges to slightly lift the crêpe and ensure the bottom is golden, then flip and cook for another 2–3 minutes.

Remove from the pan, add your filling of choice to the middle of the pancrêpe and roll it up.

SWAPSIES

Besan (chickpea flour) can be replaced with any flour of your choice or blitzed rolled oats.

STORAGE

These are best enjoyed warm out of the pan.

SERVES
2

PREP TIME
10 minutes

COOL TIME
Ideally overnight or for a minimum of 3 hours

AGE
6 months +

CHIA PUDDING – THREE WAYS

Chia seeds are bursting with fibre, protein and omega-3s. They promote healthy digestion, keep little tummies full and support brain function. Chia pudding is a nutritious treat and there are endless options for toppings. Our favourites are mango, chocolate, and berries and cream.

FOR THE BASE

2 cups milk of choice

5 tablespoons chia seeds

½ teaspoon ground cinnamon

2 teaspoons honey*

**Omit for babies under 12 months.*

FOR THE MANGO VERSION

1 cup mango, diced

Squeeze of lime juice

FOR THE CHOCOLATE VERSION

2 tablespoons raw cacao powder*

**24 months +*

FOR THE BERRIES AND CREAM VERSION

¼ cup Berry good jam (page 275)

FOR THE MANGO VERSION

Blitz the mango, lime and milk (from the base) in a blender until smooth.

Divide the mango mixture between two small containers or jars along with the remaining base ingredients. Place the lids on and shake until well combined.

Chill in the fridge for at least 3 hours. Make sure to give the mixture another good shake before serving to ensure the chia seeds are distributed throughout.

FOR THE CHOCOLATE VERSION

Divide the cacao powder and all the base ingredients between two containers or jars, place the lids on and shake until well combined.

Chill in the fridge for at least 3 hours. Make sure to give the mixture another good shake before serving.

Top with ground sunflower seeds/walnuts/cashews and your nut butter of choice.

FOR THE BERRIES AND CREAM VERSION

Divide the base ingredients between two containers or jars, place the lids on and shake until well combined.

Split the jam layer between your containers and then fill up with the rest of the chia base.

Chill in the fridge for at least 3 hours.

STORAGE

Store in the fridge for up to 5 days.

AGE
18 months +

SERVES
Makes 3½ cups

PREP TIME
10 minutes

COOK TIME
30 minutes

BABLE CEREAL

- 1 cup rolled oats
- 1 cup puffed quinoa or puffed rice
- ⅓ cup blended or finely chopped cashews
- ⅓ cup mixed sunflower and pumpkin seeds
- ⅓ cup desiccated coconut
- 1 teaspoon ground cinnamon
- 2 tablespoons coconut oil
- 1 tablespoons maple syrup/honey*
- 3 tablespoons tahini

**Omit honey for babies under 12 months.*

TO SERVE

Top with yoghurt or kefir, our Berry good jam (page 275), nut butter and your favourite fruits.

Pour your milk of choice over the cereal a few minutes before serving to soften it.

Say good morning to your little one's new favourite breakfast cereal. This cereal is superior to most supermarket options as it's packed with wholegrains, nuts and seeds, and isn't loaded with sugar. It's the perfect balanced meal, packed with fibre, to keep your family fuller for longer, will support blood-sugar levels and has a range of beautiful nutrients such as calcium, zinc, iron and magnesium.

Preheat the oven to 180°C (360°F).

Mix the dry ingredients together in a large bowl.

In a small saucepan over a low heat, combine the coconut oil, maple syrup and tahini and stir for a few minutes until melted and combined.

Pour the wet mixture over the dry mix and stir until well combined.

Spread the cereal out on a baking tray lined with baking paper and bake for 30 minutes, stirring every 10 minutes to avoid the top burning. Remove once the cereal is golden all over.

SWAPSIES

To make the cereal nut-free, omit the cashews.

Any nuts can replace the cashews, we particularly like walnuts.

To make the cereal sesame-free, swap the tahini for a nut butter of choice, such as peanut or almond butter.

STORAGE

Store in the pantry for up to 2 weeks in an airtight container or in the freezer for up to 3 months.

SERVES
4

PREP TIME
10 minutes

COOK TIME
10 minutes

AGE
6 months +

   20

BREKKY-BAKED EGGS

Our version of shakshuka is a versatile, protein-packed dish that can be enjoyed for breakfast, lunch or dinner. Serve it family-style with a side of toast to mop up the delicious sauce. It's a great way to introduce your little one to new flavours while also providing a wholesome and balanced meal for the whole family.

- 2 tablespoons extra-virgin olive oil
- 1 brown onion, diced
- 3 garlic cloves, minced
- 1 teaspoon paprika
- 1 tablespoon tomato paste (concentrated purée)
- ½ cup chopped cherry tomatoes
- 400 g (14 oz) tinned tomatoes
- 4 eggs
- 1–2 tablespoon Zesty pesto (page 271) or chopped parsley

Heat the extra-virgin olive oil in a deep frying pan over a medium heat. Sauté the onion and garlic until translucent. Add the paprika and tomato paste and stir until combined.

Stir in the cherry tomatoes and let them cook down for a minute before adding the tinned tomatoes.

Let the sauce simmer for a further 5 minutes. Create four divets in the sauce and crack in the eggs.

Add the pesto or parsley and season, if desired.

Place the lid on and turn the pan down to a low heat for 6 minutes, or until the egg whites and yolks are fully cooked.

TO SERVE

Toast or Yoghurt flatbreads (page 256) and slices of avocado.

Top the eggs with cheddar cheese or goat's cheese for an extra flavour boost.

SWAPSIES

For a vegan version, swap the eggs for cannellini beans.

STORAGE

Store in the fridge for up to 3 days.

AGE
6 months +

SERVES
Makes 9 pancakes

PREP TIME
5 minutes

COOK TIME
20 minutes

EASY-FREEZEY PANCAKES

1 large overripe banana or 2 small bananas, peeled and roughly chopped
2 eggs
1 cup rolled oats

TO SERVE

Serve with your yoghurt of choice, our Berry good jam (page 275), smooth peanut butter and ground cinnamon.

This quick and easy three-ingredient pancake recipe is perfect for the mornings you're craving pancakes but you're not up for the admin that comes with them. From freezer to table in minutes, these beautifully nourishing, fluffy pancakes will be a hit with the whole family.

Add all the ingredients to a blender and blitz until smooth.

Pour the batter into an ice-cube tray or a freezer-safe silicone mould with nine compartments.

Store in the freezer.

To prepare the pancakes, pop the frozen portions into a greased frying pan over a medium heat.

Cook for 5 minutes or until the pancakes are golden and bubbles form on top, then flip and cook for another 2–3 minutes on the other side.

SWAPSIES

For a vegan version, swap the eggs for linseed (flax seed) eggs (page 50).
Swap oats 1:1 for buckwheat flour for a gluten-free alternative.

STORAGE

Store the batter in the freezer for up to 3 months.

SERVES
2

PREP TIME
5 minutes

COOK TIME
20 minutes

AGE
24 months +

CHOCCY-BAKED OATS

Cake for breakfast? Sure, but make it healthy. Our version is oozing with antioxidants from the raw cacao, healthy fats from the chia seeds, wholegrains from the oats and natural sweetness from the banana. Who says you can't have your cake and eat it too!

- ¾ cup rolled oats
- 1 banana, peeled and roughly chopped
- 1 egg
- ½ teaspoon ground cinnamon
- 1 tablespoon raw cacao powder
- 1 tablespoon smooth peanut butter
- ¼ teaspoon baking powder
- 2 tablespoons milk of choice
- 1 tablespoon maple syrup
- 2 teaspoons chia seeds

Preheat the oven to 180°C (360°F).

Add all the ingredients to a blender and blitz until smooth.

Pour the batter into a small, ovenproof ramekin and bake in the oven for around 20 minutes.

Alternatively, you can cook the batter in the microwave in a microwave-safe dish for 2 minutes, or until the inside is a little gooey.

TO SERVE

Top with nut butter and hemp seeds. Or top the batter with choc chips before you cook it for a real chocolate hit.

STORAGE

Best enjoyed warm out of the oven.

AGE
7 months +

SERVES
Makes 6 fritters

PREP TIME
10 minutes

COOK TIME
10 minutes

CHEESY FRITZ

- 2 tablespoons extra-virgin olive oil
- ½ cup cottage cheese
- ½ cup frozen peas
- ¼ cup frozen corn
- 1 egg
- 2 tablespoons besan (chickpea flour)
- ¼ teaspoon garlic powder
- ½ teaspoon dried dill
- ½ teaspoon dried parsley
- ¼ teaspoon lemon zest

TO SERVE

Top with Guacamole (page 255) and your yoghurt of choice.

These gooey, cheesy fritters are packed with protein and calcium thanks to the cottage cheese. They also include colourful veggies that add a flavour punch and a nutritional boost to your little one's plate. Name a better way to start the day than by enjoying these protein-packed, calcium-rich and veggie-filled delights – we'll wait.

Heat the extra-virgin olive oil in a frying pan over a medium–high heat.

In a large bowl, add all the ingredients together and stir well.

Add 2 scoops of batter per fritter into the hot frying pan, making sure to leave some room between the fritters.

Flip the fritters after 3–4 minutes, or once golden, and cook for another 2–3 minutes on the other side.

SWAPSIES

Any flour would work well.

STORAGE

Store the fritters in the fridge for up to 4 days or in the freezer for up to 3 months. If freezing, separate the fritters with sheets of baking paper.

SERVES
2

PREP TIME
5 minutes

COOK TIME
7 minutes

AGE
6 months +

GREEN EGGS, NO HAM

This fluffy green spin on a traditional omelette is a great way to boost the nutrients (and we love that it's packed with veggies that can't be picked out). Another top addition is turmeric, which adds a beautiful richness and has anti-inflammatory properties. Remember to always pair turmeric with a touch of freshly ground black pepper to increase its absorption.

1 tablespoon coconut oil
¼ cup spinach
¼ cup peas
3 eggs
¼ teaspoon ground turmeric
¼ teaspoon garlic powder
Crack of freshly ground black pepper

Heat the coconut oil in a frying pan over a medium heat.

Blitz all the remaining omelette ingredients in a blender until smooth and well combined.

Pour the mixture into the hot pan and cook for about 5 minutes. If using frozen ingredients, the omelette may need longer.

Fold the omelette in half and cook for a further 2 minutes.

TO SERVE

Pair with foods rich in vitamin C like kiwi fruit, berries or our Bable baked beans (page 106).

STORAGE

This omelette is best served warm out of the frying pan but can be stored in the fridge in an airtight container for up to 3 days.

PRAM PLEASERS

AGE
18 months +

SERVES
Makes 16 balls

PREP TIME
15 minutes

COOL TIME
30 minutes

THREE-INGREDIENT POWER BALLS

- 6 medjool dates, pitted
- 400 g (14 oz) tin chickpeas, drained and patted dry with paper towel
- ½ cup tahini

These power balls are made from just three simple wholefoods. They're packed with calcium from the tahini – the hero ingredient – as well as protein, fibre and antioxidants. The dates add a nice natural sweetness so they're a sweet snack you can feel good about serving.

Cover the dates with boiling water in a bowl and soak for 1–2 minutes before draining.

Blend the chickpeas, tahini and dates in a food processor until a smooth consistency forms.

Roll the mixture into balls using your hands.

Place the balls on a lined baking tray and leave to set in the freezer for 30 minutes.

SWAPSIES

Tahini can be swapped out for any nut butter such as smooth peanut butter.

Add 2 tablespoons of chocolate chips or 2 squares of chopped good-quality dark chocolate into the mixture before you form the balls. You could also dip the balls in Choc magic shell (page 298) before freezing.

STORAGE

Store in the fridge for up to a week in an airtight container or in the freezer for up to 3 months.

SERVES
Makes 12 mini loaves or muffins

PREP TIME
10 minutes

COOK TIME
18 minutes

AGE
9 months +

NANA ZUKE BREAD

This is no ordinary banana bread – it's got the added nutritional punch of zucchini (courgette). These loaves are fluffy, moist, filled with healthy fats and protein, and are a snack toddlers and adults alike will enjoy. Add a lick of butter and you're good to go.

2 overripe bananas, peeled and roughly chopped
3 eggs
1 teaspoon vanilla extract
½ teaspoon apple-cider vinegar
3 tablespoons smooth peanut butter
¾ cup zucchini (courgette), finely grated and drained
2 cups almond meal
¼ cup arrowroot flour
1 teaspoon baking powder

Preheat the oven to 180°C (360°F).

Grease a mini loaf (bar) tin or muffin tin with oil of choice.

In a large bowl, mash the bananas with a fork.

Mix the wet ingredients into the mashed bananas.

Once combined, add all the dry ingredients to the bowl and stir. Pour mixture into the loaf (bar) tin.

Bake for 16–18 minutes, or until a knife inserted in the middle of the loaves comes out clean.

Remove from the oven and let cool in the tin for a few minutes. Let the loaves cool completely on a wire rack before serving.

SWAPSIES

Peanut butter can be swapped for any nut or seed butter of choice.

Swap out almond meal for whole-wheat flour.

Arrowroot flour can be swapped out for any other flour such as tapioca or oat flour.

Add 2 tablespoons of maple syrup for little ones over 18 months for a sweeter option.

If you choose to make it in a big loaf tin, bake for 30–40 minutes.

STORAGE

Store at room temperature for 3 days in an airtight container or in the freezer for up to 3 months.

AGE
24 months +

SERVES
Makes 20 balls

PREP TIME
10 minutes

ZESTY LAMINGTON BALLS

12 medjool dates, pitted
¼ cup raw cacao powder
¼ cup orange juice, freshly squeezed
½ teaspoon orange rind
1 teaspoon ground cinnamon
2 tablespoons chia seeds
½ cup mixed sunflower and pepita seeds (pumpkin seeds)
1 cup desiccated coconut
⅔ cup ground linseed (flax seed)
1 teaspoon vanilla extract
Pinch of salt

These zesty lamington bliss balls are not only a convenient and portable lunchbox-friendly snack but also a great source of energy, antioxidants and essential nutrients. These balls are easy to throw together so whip them up and stash in your bag for those moments you need an emergency snack on hand.

Cover the dates in boiling water and soak for 1–2 minutes to soften.

Drain the dates and add them to a food processor with the remaining ingredients (reserving ¼ cup of coconut for decorating) and blend until well combined.

Roll the mixture into balls.

Sprinkle ¼ cup of desiccated coconut on a plate and roll each ball in the coconut to finish.

SWAPSIES

Ground linseed (flax seed) can be swapped for LSA (linseed, sunflower seed and almond meal). However be mindful that LSA contains nuts.

STORAGE

Store in fridge for up to 2 weeks in an airtight container or in the freezer for up to 3 months.

SERVING SIZE
Makes 12 balls

PREP TIME
15 minutes

AGE
12 months +

RED VELVET BALLS

These balls are rich in iron and vitamin C because of the hero ingredient, beetroot (beet). They're a great quick snack that can be pre-prepared and pulled from the freezer at a moment's notice. Sweet and coconutty, they're a fun way to get beetroot into your little one's diet and if you poke a paper straw through the bottom of them, you have cake pops – always a big hit at parties!

- 10 medjool dates, pitted
- 125 g (4½ oz) pre-cooked beetroot (beet)
- ¾ cup desiccated coconut
- 1 cup rolled oats
- 2 tablespoons ground linseed (flax seed)

Cover the dates with boiling water in a bowl and soak for 1–2 minutes before draining.

Blend the dates, beetroot, ½ cup of the desiccated coconut, the rolled oats and ground linseed (flax seed) in a food processor until well combined.

Roll the mixture into balls. Depending on how big you form them, this recipe should make approximately 12 balls.

Sprinkle the remaining desiccated coconut on a plate and roll each ball in the coconut to finish.

SWAPSIES

The ground linseed (flax seed) can be replaced with almond meal.

You can roll the balls in lots of different ingredients including hemp seeds, blended nuts, freeze-dried raspberries, raw cacao powder, or dip them in melted chocolate.

STORAGE

Store in the fridge for up to 3 days in an airtight container or in the freezer for up to 3 months.

AGE
12 months +

SERVES
12 medium muffins or 16 mini muffins

PREP TIME
10 minutes

COOK TIME
14–18 minutes

TURBO MUFFINS

- 3 overripe bananas, peeled and roughly chopped
- 2 cups rolled oats
- 2 eggs
- 1 teaspoon apple-cider vinegar
- ⅓ cup Date paste (page 268)
- ½ teaspoon baking powder
- ½ teaspoon bicarbonate of soda (baking soda)
- 1 teaspoon vanilla extract

TOPPINGS

Choc chips, raspberries, sliced banana

We've dubbed these turbo muffins because they're not only turbocharged with wholefoods but they're also super speedy to make! They're full of fibre and only natural sugars so they're a great toddler snack. Get your little ones to decorate the muffins with their favourite toppings. This batch will make enough to enjoy fresh with extras to freeze for quick brekkies or lunchboxes.

Preheat the oven to 180°C (360°F).

Blend all the ingredients together in a food processor or blender until well combined.

Grease your muffin moulds and divide your batter between 12 muffin moulds or 16 mini moulds.

Top each muffin with a sprinkle of choc chips, raspberries or sliced banana.

Bake for 14–18 minutes, or until golden brown and a knife inserted in the middle comes out clean.

Leave to cool for 10 minutes before removing from the muffin tin. Transfer to a wire rack to cool.

SWAPSIES

Try other toppings like apple slices and ground cinnamon or a dollop of Berry good jam (page 275).

Date paste can be swapped with ¼ cup maple syrup.

STORAGE

Store for up to 5 days in the fridge in an airtight container or in the freezer for up to 3 months.

SERVES
8

PREP TIME
10 minutes

COOK TIME
40–50 minutes

AGE
18 months +

BERRY GOOD BANANA BREAD

This delicious banana bread is not only a crowd pleaser but also a nutritious snack packed with protein. The overripe bananas add natural sweetness without the need for added sugars and the besan (chickpea flour) amps up the protein so everyone stays fuller for longer. With the addition of juicy berries, each bite bursts with fruity goodness and antioxidants.

3 overripe bananas, peeled and roughly chopped

2 eggs, lightly beaten

1 teaspoon vanilla extract

1 teaspoon apple-cider vinegar

3 tablespoons maple syrup

¼ cup extra-virgin olive oil

1½ cups besan (chickpea flour)

½ teaspoon ground cinnamon

½ teaspoon bicarbonate of soda (baking soda)

½ teaspoon baking powder

1 cup berries (fresh or frozen)

Preheat the oven to 180°C (360°F).

Line a medium-sized loaf (bar) tin with baking paper.

In a large bowl, mash up the bananas and then mix with the eggs, vanilla, apple-cider vinegar, maple syrup and olive oil.

Add the dry ingredients and mix until well combined.

Fold in the berries (leaving a few aside for decorating with before they go in the oven).

Pour the mixture into your prepared loaf tin and bake for 40–50 minutes, or until a knife inserted in the middle comes out clean.

TO SERVE

Add a lick of butter or nut butter.

SWAPSIES

Swap besan (chickpea flour) for flour of choice.

STORAGE

Store at room temperature or in the fridge for up to 3 days in an airtight container or in the freezer for up to 3 months. Defrost and warm through before serving.

AGE
12 months +

SERVES
Makes 15 balls

PREP TIME
10 minutes

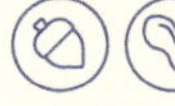   

NUTTY COOKIE DOUGH BALLS

- 5 medjool dates, pitted
- ¾ cup rolled oats
- 1 cup almond meal
- 1 tablespoon chia seeds
- 3 tablespoons coconut oil, melted
- ½ cup smooth peanut butter
- ¼ teaspoon ground cinnamon
- 1 tablespoon choc chips (optional)

These naturally sweetened peanut butter cookie balls are our healthy alternative to a traditional cookie. They're full of good fats, fibre and lots of protein so they will keep your little one's belly satisfied. These are as yummy as a regular cookie, but they'll leave you feeling much better. They are Just. That. Good.

Cover the dates with boiling water in a bowl and soak for a minute before draining.

Blitz the oats in a food processor for 10 seconds or until a floury consistency forms.

Add all the other ingredients to the oat flour and blend until a smooth dough forms.

Scoop out 1 tablespoon for each ball and roll. This should make approximately 15 balls.

STORAGE

Store in the fridge for up to 2 weeks in an airtight container or in the freezer for up to 3 months.

SWAPSIES

Add choc chips before rolling for a sweet addition or drizzle with our Choc magic shell (page 298).

SERVES
Makes 9 balls

PREP TIME
5 minutes

AGE
12 months +

APRICOT DELIGHTS

These lunchbox-friendly snack balls are truly a delight – in just 5 minutes you can create a delicious and wholesome snack. They are bursting with healthy fats and omega-3s from the chia seeds and hemp seeds, and iron from the dried apricots. They're also a great snack to keep in the fridge for when you want something indulgent but not too sweet.

5 medjool dates, pitted
¾ cup desiccated coconut
½ cup dried sulphur-free apricots
1 tablespoon chia seeds
1 tablespoon hemp seeds

Cover the dates with boiling water in a bowl and soak for 1–2 minutes before draining.

Blend all the ingredients (reserving ¼ cup of desiccated coconut for decorating) in a food processor until a smooth dough forms.

Scoop out 1 tablespoon for each ball and roll with damp hands. This recipe should make approximately 9 balls.

Sprinkle the remaining desiccated coconut onto a plate and roll each ball in the coconut to finish.

SWAPSIES

Add choc chips before rolling for a sweet addition or drizzle with our Choc magic shell (page 298).

STORAGE

Store in the fridge for up to 2 weeks in an airtight container or in the freezer for up to 3 months.

AGE
6 months +

SERVES
Makes 20 bite-sized gummies

PREP TIME
5 minutes

COOK TIME
10 minutes

COOL TIME
3 hours

BERRY YUMMY GUMMIES

1 cup berries of choice (fresh or frozen)
1½ tablespoons chia seeds
½ cup boiling water

FOR THE GELATIN
2½ tablespoons gelatin
120 ml (4 fl oz) cold water

TO SERVE

Cut into finger-shaped pieces for babies aged 6–9 months.

These homemade gummies are a fantastic addition to your little one's diet. The chia seeds have omega-3s and fibre, the berries provide an antioxidant boost and let's not forget about the gelatin! Derived from collagen, gelatin is a superfood for gut health and immune function. Your little one will love these gummies and you can feel confident knowing they're a tasty snack that also nourishes their growing body.

Stir the berries, chia seeds and boiling water together in a small saucepan over a medium heat. After a few minutes, turn the heat down to low and let the mixture cook for another 5 minutes until the chia seeds swell. Mash well with a fork then take the saucepan off the heat.

In a small bowl, add the gelatin powder and cold water and stir for 30 seconds or until the gelatin 'blooms' (this just means it swells and looks a bit fluffy).

Add the gelatin to the saucepan, stirring for another minute until well combined and the gelatin has completely melted.

Carefully pour the mixture into your moulds of choice. We like using fun-shaped moulds or you can use a silicone loaf tin or a shallow dish and slice into squares once the gummies have set.

Place in the fridge for at least 3 hours to set then transfer to an airtight container.

SWAPSIES

Reduce gelatine mixture to 2 tablespoons and 80 ml (2½ fl oz/⅓ cup) or just ⅓ cup cold water to soften the texture for little ones under 12 months.

STORAGE

Store in the fridge for up to 7 days in an airtight container.

SERVES
Makes 10 cookies

PREP TIME
5 minutes

COOK TIME
10–15 minutes

AGE
12 months +

GOOEY CHICKPEA COOKIES

A great alternative to a traditional cookie is our protein-packed chickpea version filled with ingredients you most likely already have in the pantry. These have a nice sweetness from the dates plus healthy fats and even more protein from the peanut butter. These yummy cookies are so nutrient-dense, you'll want your little one asking for more, more, more!

6 medjool dates, pitted

400 g (14 oz) tin chickpeas, drained, rinsed and patted dry with paper towel

½ cup smooth peanut butter

½ teaspoon baking powder

1–2 tablespoons chocolate chips (optional)

Preheat the oven to 180°C (360°F).

Cover the dates with boiling water in a bowl and soak for 1–2 minutes before draining.

Blend all the ingredients, except the chocolate chips, in a food processor until well combined.

Stir in the chocolate chips.

With damp hands, roll the mixture into ten balls then place them on a baking tray lined with baking paper and flatten with a fork or with your fingers.

Bake for 12–15 minutes or until golden.

Transfer to a wire rack and leave to cool for 10 minutes.

SWAPSIES

Chocolate chips can be swapped for chopped dates or raisins.

For a nut-free option, swap out the peanut butter for tahini.

STORAGE

Store at room temperature for up to 2 weeks in an airtight container.

AGE
12 months +

SERVES
Makes 9 cookies

PREP TIME
5 minutes

COOK TIME
15 minutes

EASY-PEASY COOKIES

- 2 overripe bananas, peeled and mashed
- 2 cups rolled oats
- 2 tablespoons smooth peanut butter

These simple oat cookies are the answer when you have ripe bananas sitting on your counter. With just three ingredients, they deliver a powerful combination of protein, healthy fats and carbohydrates. You can whip up a batch in no time and then enjoy having a delicious snack that will keep you and your little one fuelled throughout the day.

Preheat the oven to 180°C (360°F).

Mix all the ingredients together in a large bowl until well combined.

Roll the mixture into nine balls then place them on a baking tray lined with baking paper and flatten with a fork or with your fingers.

Bake for 12–15 minutes or until golden brown.

Transfer to a wire rack and leave to cool for 10 minutes.

SWAPSIES

For a nut-free option, swap out the peanut butter for tahini.

STORAGE

Store at room temperature for up to a week in an airtight container.

SERVES
Makes approximately 20 crackers

PREP TIME
5 minutes

COOK TIME
40 minutes

AGE
18 months +

CRUNCHY SEED SNAPS

Toddlers love a cracker and these homemade seed crackers are a nutrient powerhouse! They contain omega-3s and antioxidants, and are the perfect alternative to processed crackers from the supermarket. Pair them with cheese slices or your favourite dip and enjoy the satisfying crunch.

½ cup sunflower seeds
½ cup pepita (pumpkin seed)
¼ cup linseed (flax seed)
¼ cup chia seeds
¼ cup sesame seeds
1 teaspoon dried herbs of choice (we use rosemary or oregano)
1 cup water

TO SERVE

Dip into some Pink hummus (page 272), Zesty pesto (page 271), Guacamole (page 255), or serve with cheese slices.

Preheat the oven to 180°C (360°F).

Mix all the dry ingredients together in a large bowl until well combined.

Stir in the water then place the mixture in the fridge for 15–20 minutes to thicken.

Once the mixture has a gel-like consistency, pour it onto a baking tray lined with baking paper.

Take another piece of baking paper the same size as the tray and place it on top of the mixture. Press down with your hands or the side of a cup or a rolling pin. Try and flatten out the seed mixture as much as possible, aiming for a consistent thickness from the middle to the edges.

Bake in the oven for 30 minutes.

Remove the tray from the oven, let it cool for a few minutes, break with your hands or cut the crackers with a knife into small pieces, the size of your choosing.

Flip the crackers over and bake for another 10 minutes or until both sides are golden and crisp.

SWAPSIES

For a sesame-free version, replace the sesame seeds with an extra tablespoon of all the other ingredients.

STORAGE

Store at room temperature for up to 2 weeks in an airtight container or in the freezer for up to 3 months.

AGE
18 months +

SERVES
Makes 12 bites

PREP TIME
8 minutes

COOK TIME
12 minutes

   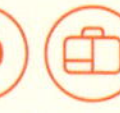  

MUNCHY MUESLI BITES

- 4 medjool dates, pitted and finely chopped
- ¼ cup coconut oil
- ¼ cup tahini
- ¼ cup maple syrup or honey*
- 2 cups rolled oats
- ½ cup roughly chopped mixed sunflower and pepita seeds (pumpkin seeds)
- ¼ cup desiccated coconut
- ¼ cup spelt flour
- Pinch of salt (optional)

**Omit for babies under 12 months.*

TO SERVE

Melt some dark chocolate, carob or Choc magic shell (page 298) and drizzle over the top and set in the freezer for at least an hour.

Introducing the ultimate lunchbox-friendly snack: our delicious nut-free muesli bites! Made with a delightful combination of tahini, oats, a mix of sunflower and pepita (pumpkin seed), desiccated coconut and medjool dates, these muesli bites are pure goodness. To make them even more appealing, add a drizzle of chocolate on top.

Preheat the oven to 160°C (320°F).

Cover the dates with boiling water in a bowl and soak for 1–2 minutes before draining.

Add the coconut oil, tahini and maple syrup to a small saucepan over a low heat and stir until everything is combined.

Meanwhile, mix your dry ingredients together in a large bowl.

Pour the wet ingredients into the dry mix and stir until well combined.

Spoon the mixture into a silicone muffin tray. We like the mini ones for little bites. Pat it down as much as possible with the back of a spoon or your fingers to ensure they are tightly packed.

Bake for 12 minutes, or until a knife inserted in the middle of a bite the middle comes out clean.

Remove the tray from the oven and leave to cool for 10 minutes before removing the bites from the moulds. Transfer to a wire rack to cool.

SWAPSIES

For a vegan version, swap the honey for maple syrup.

For a wheat-free version, swap the spelt flour for a wheat-free flour like besan (chickpea flour).

STORAGE

Store at room temperature for up to 2 weeks in an airtight container or in the freezer for up to 3 months.

SERVES
Makes 12 muffins

PREP TIME
10 minutes

COOK TIME
20 minutes

AGE
12 months +

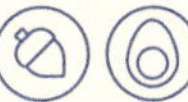

THUMBPRINT MUFFINS

These are one of our favourite recipes and our toddlers are obsessed! These fluffy muffins are sweetened with overripe bananas, a touch of maple syrup and our Berry good jam.

- 3 overripe bananas, peeled and roughly chopped
- 2 cups almond meal
- 2 eggs
- 1 teaspoon apple-cider vinegar
- 1 tablespoon maple syrup
- 1 teaspoon vanilla extract
- 1 teaspoon baking powder
- ⅓ cup Berry good jam (page 275)

Preheat the oven to 180°C (360°F).

Add all the ingredients, except the chia jam, to a bowl and stir until well combined.

Add half of the mixture into a greased 12-hole muffin tin or silicone mould.

Add 1 teaspoon of chia jam to the top of each muffin then spoon in the remaining mixture to cover each portion so the chia jam is sandwiched between the muffin layers.

Add another ½ teaspoon or whatever is left of your chia jam to top each muffin off.

Bake in the oven for 20 minutes, or until a knife inserted in the middle of a muffin comes out clean.

Leave to cool for 10 minutes on a wire rack.

SWAPSIES

For a nut-free version, swap the almond meal for rolled oats.

STORAGE

Store in the fridge for up to 5 days in an airtight container or in the freezer for up to 3 months.

AGE
6 months +

SERVES
Makes 20 gummies (mould size dependent)

PREP TIME
5 minutes

COOK TIME
25 minutes

COOL TIME
3 hours

CREAMY MANGO SQUISHIES

COCONUT LAYER
270 ml coconut milk
1 teaspoon vanilla extract
1½ tablespoons gelatin
3 tablespoons cold water
1 tablespoon honey*

MANGO LAYER
1½ cups frozen mango
¾ cup boiling water
3 tablespoons gelatin
120 ml (4 fl oz) cold water
**Omit honey for babies under 12 months.*

TO SERVE

Cut into finger-shaped pieces for babies aged 6–9 months.

STORAGE

Store in the fridge for up to 7 days in an airtight container.

Not only are these mango squishies delicious and creamy, but they also offer a range of nutritional benefits. The addition of gelatin provides valuable gut health benefits, while the inclusion of coconut milk offers a dose of healthy fats.

For the coconut layer, add the coconut milk and vanilla extract to a saucepan over a low–medium heat and stir to combine.

While the coconut milk is heating, add the gelatin and of cold water to a small bowl and stir for 30 seconds until it blooms.

Add the gelatin to the saucepan and stir until the gelatin has melted. Let cool for a few minutes and stir in the honey, if including.

Fill your moulds of choice one-quarter of the way with the coconut mixture. Place in the fridge and set for 20 minutes.

Meanwhile, blitz the mango and boiling water in a blender until smooth.

Rinse your saucepan and return to the heat. Heat the mango mixture over a low–medium heat, stirring often.

Repeat the gelatin step above for the mango layer, but this time add 3 tablespoons of gelatin powder and 120 ml (4 fl oz) cold water. Stir for 30 seconds until it blooms.

Add the gelatin to the mango pot, stirring until well combined and the gelatin has melted.

Once the coconut layer has had 20 minutes to set, pour your mango mixture into the moulds over the coconut mixture.

Note: If you can't wait 20 minutes between layers, just pour the mango mixture in as soon as it's ready and you'll get more of a marbled effect.

Place into the fridge for at least 3 hours to set and transfer to an airtight container.

SERVES
2

PREP TIME
5 minutes

AGE
24 months +

  20 

CHOCOLATE THICKSHAKE

2 teaspoons raw cacao powder
½ cup frozen cauliflower
½ cup frozen zucchini (courgette)
1 large frozen banana
¼ cup yoghurt of choice
1 tablespoon hemp seeds
1 tablespoon smooth peanut butter
¾ cup milk of choice
2 medjool dates, pitted
Handful of ice
1 tablespoon grass-fed collagen powder (optional)

You would never guess this delicious chocolate thickshake is packed with veggies. It's filled with antioxidants from the cacao; healthy fats and protein from the yoghurt, hemp seeds and peanut butter; and the cauliflower and zucchini (courgette) adds creaminess and lots of goodness!

Add all the ingredients to a blender and blitz until smooth.

SWAPSIES

For a nut-free version, omit the peanut butter.

STORAGE

Leftovers can be stored in the fridge for a day.

AGE
6 months +

SERVES
2

PREP TIME
5 minutes

SUPERHERO SMOOTHIE

1 frozen banana
¼ cup avocado
½ cup frozen spinach
½ pear
1¼ cups milk of choice
1 tablespoon hemp seeds
1 tablespoon cashew nuts
1 medjool date, pitted
¼ cup frozen zucchini (courgette)
Handful of ice

When it comes to smoothies, we say the more the merrier. They're a great way to get extra nutrients into your little one's diet, especially during the fussy toddler years. Slurping on smoothies can be a fun, refreshing and delicious way to ensure your little one gets the nutrients they need. This one is filled with green goodness – it's sweet, creamy and has lots of veggies!

Add all the ingredients to a blender and blitz until smooth.

SWAPSIES

For a nut-free version, omit the cashews.

STORAGE

Leftovers can be store in the fridge for a day or turned into Smoothie pops (page 302).

SERVES
2

PREP TIME
5 minutes

AGE
6 months +

BERRY BLAST SMOOTHIE

Our go-to berry smoothie is a great way to start the day. Loaded with berries, it's a powerhouse of antioxidants and vitamin C, which support immune health. It also has protein-rich collagen, peanut butter and hemp seeds to keep your little one full and happy.

- 1 overripe banana, peeled and roughly chopped
- ¼ cup frozen spinach
- ⅓ cup frozen berries
- ⅓ cup rolled oats
- 1 tablespoon smooth peanut butter
- 1 tablespoon hemp seeds
- 1 medjool date, pitted
- ½ teaspoon ground cinnamon
- 1 cup milk of choice
- Handful of ice
- 1 tablespoon grass-fed collagen powder (optional)
- 1 tablespoon linseed (flax seed) oil (optional)

Add all the ingredients to a blender and blitz until smooth.

SWAPSIES

For a peanut-free version, swap peanut butter for a nut or seed butter or omit completely.

STORAGE

Leftovers can be stored in the fridge for a day.

AGE
12 months +

SERVES
Makes 12 mini muffins

PREP TIME
15 minutes

COOK TIME
15 minutes

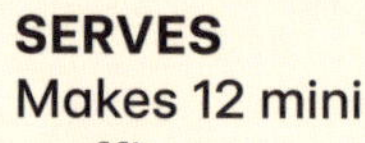

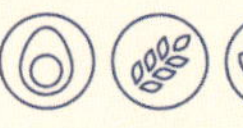

MIGHTY VEGGIE MUFFINS

- ½ cup zucchini (courgette), finely grated and drained
- 1 cup sweet potato, finely grated and squeezed
- ½ cup frozen peas
- 2 eggs
- ¼ cup milk of choice
- 1 teaspoon apple-cider vinegar
- ¼ cup extra-virgin olive oil
- ¾ cup cheddar cheese, grated
- 1 cup spelt flour
- ½ teaspoon bicarbonate of soda (baking soda)
- ½ teaspoon baking powder
- ¼ teaspoon dried basil
- ¼ teaspoon dried oregano
- ½ teaspoon thyme
- 1 garlic clove, minced

These fluffy, cheesy veggie muffins are such a perfect snack and a yummy way to celebrate vegetables.

The combination of grated zucchini (courgette), sweet potato and peas provides a variety of vitamins and minerals to support your little one's growth. They're made with spelt flour, which is a great replacement for refined white flour and the eggs and cheese ensure they're a good source of protein too.

Preheat the oven to 180°C (360°F).

Add all the ingredients to a large bowl (reserving ¼ cup of cheese) and stir until well combined.

Grease a 12-hole mini muffin tray or use silicone moulds.

Pour the mixture into the tray and top with the remaining grated cheese. Bake for 15 minutes, or until golden on top and a knife inserted into the middle of a muffin comes out clean.

Turn the muffins out of the tray and let them cool on a wire rack for 10 minutes before enjoying.

SWAPSIES

Spelt flour can be swapped 1:1 with another flour of choice.

Swap peas with corn or a veggie medley mix.

Swap sweet potato with pumpkin (squash).

STORAGE

Store in the fridge for up to 5 days in an airtight container or in the freezer for up to 3 months.

SERVES
Makes 6 muffins or 12 mini bites

PREP TIME
10 minutes

COOK TIME
30 minutes

AGE
7 months +

EGG POPPERS

These delectable bites are not only simple to whip up but are a very convenient snack to take on-the-go when you're rushing out of the house. Packed with choline, a nutrient essential for brain development and loaded with a variety of veggies, they provide a wholesome dose of vitamins and minerals. The feta and dill combo adds a punch of flavour in each bite. These taste so yummy straight out of the oven, even the little food critics will love them!

½ cup cherry tomatoes, quartered

½ cup frozen peas

¼ cup feta

2 garlic cloves, minced

2 teaspoons dried dill

4 eggs

Preheat the oven to 180°C (360°F).

Mix together the cherry tomatoes, peas, feta, garlic and dill in a large mixing bowl, making sure to squash the peas if your little one is under 12 months.

Spoon the mixture evenly into a greased 6-hole muffin tin or 12-hole mini muffin tin.

In a separate bowl, crack in the eggs and whisk until well combined.

Pour the eggs evenly on top of the mixture.

Bake for 20–30 minutes or until the poppers are cooked through.

Leave to cool for 10 minutes before serving.

SWAPSIES

Feta is a high-sodium cheese so you may want to swap it for cottage cheese for babies under 12 months.

Try dried oregano instead of dill.

Most veggies will work here: we also like using capsicum (bell pepper) or spinach.

STORAGE

Store in the fridge for up to 3 days in an airtight container or in the freezer for up to 3 months.

AGE
6 months +

SERVES
Makes 12 gummies

PREP TIME
2 minutes

COOK TIME
5 minutes

COOL TIME
3 hours +

SUPERCHARGED SQUISHIES

1 cup freshly squeezed orange juice
2 tablespoons lemon juice
½ teaspoon finely grated fresh ginger
⅛ teaspoon ground turmeric
Pinch of finely ground black pepper
2½ tablespoons gelatin
100 ml (3½ fl oz) filtered water
1 teaspoon honey*
**Omit honey for babies under 12 months.*

TO SERVE

Cut into finger-shaped pieces for babies aged 6–9 months.

Bursting with the tangy flavours of orange and lemon, these gummies are packed with vitamin C to support the immune system and ward off seasonal bugs. We've also added ginger and turmeric to help reduce inflammation and soothe sore throats. These powerful ingredients boast antibacterial properties, providing an extra layer of protection against viruses. Say hello to winter with confidence, knowing that you're equipped with the perfect sweet-and-sour squishies to help your family stay well.

Add orange juice, lemon juice, grated ginger, turmeric and a pinch of pepper to a small saucepan over a low–medium heat and stir until combined.

Meanwhile, add the gelatin and filtered water to a small bowl and stir for 30 seconds until the gelatin blooms.

Pour the gelatin mixture into the saucepan, stirring for another minute or so until the gelatin has melted. Allow to cool for a few minutes before mixing in the honey.

Carefully pour the mixture into your moulds of choice and allow to set in the fridge for at least 3 hours before transferring to an airtight container.

STORAGE

Store in the fridge for up to a week in an airtight container.

SERVES
Makes 3 large pops or 5 small pops

PREP TIME
10 minutes

COOL TIME
4 hours

AGE
6 months +

BROTH BLOCKS

This is a clever way to get broth into your little one's tummy as the taste of the broth is extremely subtle! Oozing with collagen, gut goodness, anti-inflammatory properties and protein, this is a homemade icy treat you will feel excited about offering.

⅔ cup Hug-in-a-cup broth (page 279), cooled

½ cup coconut milk

1 cup frozen mixed berries

2 teaspoons maple syrup

Pinch of sea salt (optional)

Add all the ingredients to a blender and blitz until smooth.

Pour into your moulds of choice and set in the freezer for at least 4 hours.

SWAPSIES

For babies under 12 months omit the maple syrup and salt.

Fresh berries can be used instead of frozen. Berries can also be swapped 1:1 for frozen mango.

STORAGE

Store in the freezer for up to 3 months.

LUNCH BOXES

LUNCHBOXES

These 20 balanced, wholesome and nut-free lunchboxes will be loved by your little one.

LUNCHBOX 1

+ Pretzels
+ Three-ingredient power ball (page 132)
+ Pear slices, raspberries and cucumber slices
+ Corn on the cob
+ Easy-peasy crêpes (page 105) filled with ricotta and lemon zest

LUNCHBOX 2

+ Bouncy brekky bite (page 101)
+ Pitted date
+ Mix of tomato, avocado, cucumber sticks and olives (quartered)
+ Freeze-dried apples
+ Pasta with Secret sauce (page 209)

LUNCHBOX 3

+ Strawberries
+ Apricot delight (page 147)
+ Pickles and avocado with hemp seeds
+ Cheesy fritz (page 126)
+ Rice cakes with Seed butter (page 267)

LUNCHBOX 4

+ Cantaloupe fingers
+ Munchy muesli bite (page 156)
+ Avo and cheese on crackers
+ Celery
+ Falafel bites (page 192) and hummus

LUNCHBOX 5

+ Roasted chickpeas
+ Fruit straps
+ Corn and peas
+ Strawberries and blueberries
+ Quesadillas with avocado, cheese and Meatballs and veggie sauce (page 234)

1

2

4
3
5

LUNCHBOX 6

+ Apple slices
+ Grated cheddar cheese
+ Steamed broccoli and grated carrot
+ Monster pancakes (page 94)
+ Quinoa wrap (page 263) with Super sardine bites (page 191) and avocado

LUNCHBOX 7

+ Pickles
+ Berry yummy gummies (page 148)
+ Baked sweet potato chips
+ Egg poppers (page 171)
+ Sourdough sandwich with Berry good jam (page 275)

LUNCHBOX 8

+ Bable baked beans (page 106)
+ Dried blueberries
+ Peas and baked sweet potato chips
+ Plum slices
+ Mighty veggie muffins (page 168)

LUNCHBOX 9

+ Chickpeas
+ Dried apricots
+ Seed butter (page 267) and apple sandwich
+ Seed crackers with Pink hummus (page 272)
+ Quinoa and amaranth pasta with Zesty pesto (page 271)

LUNCHBOX 10

+ Capsicum (bell pepper) sticks and tomatoes (quartered)
+ Edamame
+ Popcorn (can be a choking hazard for children under 5 years old)
+ Seed butter (page 267) sandwich on wholemeal bread
+ Yoghurt with Berry good jam (page 275)

6

7

9
8
10

LUNCHBOX 11

+ Crinkle-cut carrots
+ Supercharged squishies (page 172)
+ Salmon bites (page 188)
+ Hummus and cucumber sticks
+ Heartbeet pancakes (page 97)

LUNCHBOX 12

+ Kiwi fruit and strawberries
+ Seed and date mix
+ Cucumber, carrot and celery slices
+ Boiled eggs with cumin
+ Toasted wholegrain sandwich with cheese and tomato

11

LUNCHBOX 13

+ Dried fava beans
+ Steamed broccoli
+ Salmon, avocado and cucumber sandwich on wholegrain bread
+ Berry good jam (page 275)
+ Mandarin
+ Bable cereal (page 118) and yoghurt

LUNCHBOX 14

+ Mandarin and grapes
+ Choc chips
+ Beetroot (beet) slices, cherry tomatoes and olives (quartered)
+ Little veggie sausage rolls (page 203)
+ Hummus, cucumber and tuna wrap

LUNCHBOX 15

+ Celery sticks
+ Munchy muesli bite (page 156)
+ Toasted wholegrain sandwich with cheese and tomato
+ Banana
+ Little veggie sausage rolls (page 203)

12

14
13
15

LUNCHBOX 16

+ Kiwi fruit
+ Red velvet ball (page 139)
+ String cheese and carrot sticks
+ Gooey chickpea cookie (page 151)
+ Chips 'n' guac (page 255)

LUNCHBOX 17

+ Carrots and cucumber sticks
+ Greek yoghurt
+ Sushi (page 195)
+ Berry good banana bread (page 143)
+ Orange slices

LUNCHBOX 18

+ Raspberries
+ Seed mix
+ Seaweed
+ Turbo muffin (page 140)
+ Quinoa pasta with peas, corn, hemp seeds and extra-virgin olive oil

LUNCHBOX 19

+ Pizza (page 242)
+ Cucumber and capsicum (bell pepper) sticks
+ Boiled eggs with hemp seeds
+ Berry yummy gummies (page 148)
+ Peas with melted butter

LUNCHBOX 20

+ Quinoa rainbow rice (page 229)
+ Cucumber sticks, olives and cherry tomatoes (quartered)
+ Cheddar cheese slices
+ Pickles
+ Munchy muesli bite (page 156)
+ Apricots and blueberries

16

17

19
18
20

SMALL BITES

AGE
7 months +

SERVES
Makes 8–10 bites

PREP TIME
10 minutes

COOK TIME
10 minutes

SALMON BITES

- 415 g (14½ oz) wild tinned salmon
- 1 carrot, grated and squeezed
- 1 egg
- ¼ cup almond meal
- 1 tablespoon ground linseed (flax seed) (optional add in)
- ½ cup cooked quinoa
- 1 teaspoon paprika
- 1 teaspoon ground cumin
- ½ teaspoon garlic powder
- 1 tablespoon extra-virgin olive oil (for frying)

These salmon bites are a powerhouse of nutrition. Packed with omega-3s from the salmon, they're not only delicious but also a good source of protein. The inclusion of quinoa adds a dose of fibre and essential nutrients. We love to whip these up and stash them in the freezer for a ready-to-go nutritious meal.

Heat a frying pan over a medium heat.

In a large bowl, mix all the ingredients, except the oil, until well combined.

Roll approximately 1 tablespoon worth of the mixture into balls.

Melt the oil in a frying pan over a medium heat and add your balls to the pan, pressing them down with a fork to flatten slightly.

Cook on each side for 3–4 minutes or until golden.

SWAPSIES

For a lunchbox-friendly nut-free version, swap the almond meal for spelt flour.

STORAGE

Store in the fridge for up to 4 days in an airtight container or in the freezer for up to 3 months. If freezing, use sheets of baking paper in between each bite to avoid them sticking.

SERVES
Makes 16 bites

PREP TIME
10 minutes

COOK TIME
15 minutes

AGE
7 months +

SUPER SARDINE BITES

These sardine bites have a multitude of benefits. Sardines are a fantastic source of omega-3s, which support brain health and function while providing anti-inflammatory properties. The soft bones in sardines are also an excellent source of calcium, which contributes to strong bones and teeth. Additionally, sardines contain vitamin D, a nutrient that is often challenging to obtain through diet alone.

200 g (7 oz) tinned sardines, rinsed and drained
1 egg
½ cup cooked quinoa
2 tablespoons hemp seeds
1 teaspoon lemon rind
¼ cup grated parmesan cheese
2 tablespoons spelt flour
1 tablespoon chopped fresh parsley, or 2 teaspoons dried parsley
2 tablespoons extra-virgin olive oil (for frying)

In a large bowl, mix all the ingredients, except the oil, together until well combined. Season if desired.

Heat the oil in a large frying pan over a medium–high heat.

Roll the mixture into sixteen small balls then flatten them slightly with your hands or a fork and add to the pan.

Cook on each side for 3–4 minutes or until golden.

SWAPSIES

Spelt flour can be swapped for any flour of choice.

Swap parmesan for mozzarella for babies under 12 months.

STORAGE

Store in the fridge for up to 4 days or in the freezer for up 3 months.

AGE
6 months +

SERVES
Makes 16 bites

PREP TIME
10 minutes

COOK TIME
10–15 minutes

   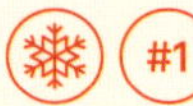 

FALAFEL BITES

- 400 g (14 oz) dried chickpeas*, soaked overnight (see page 79 for soaking instructions)
- ½ cup parsley leaves
- ½ cup coriander (cilantro) leaves
- ½ brown onion, diced
- 1 teaspoon ground cumin
- 4 garlic cloves, peeled
- 2 tablespoons besan (chickpea flour)
- ½ teaspoon bicarbonate of soda (baking soda)
- 1 teaspoon lemon zest
- ½ teaspoon salt
- 1 tablespoon extra-virgin olive oil (for frying)

**Tinned chickpeas create a very different texture so we don't recommend using them in this recipe.*

TO SERVE

Serve with hummus, cucumber sticks, tahini or yoghurt dip and a side of veggies.

FIRST FOOD

Cut the falafels into finger-shaped pieces.

These bites are a great way to pack legumes and fresh herbs into your little one's diet. They're a beautiful plant-based protein option packed with flavour, antioxidants and prebiotics. Add some hummus and you have a winning combo!

Add all the ingredients, except the oil, to a food processor and blend until well combined.

Roll the falafel mix into sixteen balls.

Heat the oil in a frying pan over a medium–high heat.

Add the falafels to the pan and flatten them slightly with a fork. Let them cook on each side for 5 minutes or until golden.

STORAGE

Store in the fridge for up to a week in an airtight container or in the freezer for up to 6 months.

SWAPSIES

Omit salt for under 12 months.

SERVES
Makes 24 pieces

PREP TIME
10 minutes

COOK TIME
20 minutes

AGE
18 months +

SUSHI

Bulk the rolls up with some protein and you have a beautiful balanced meal or fill them with avocado as a snack or side. Nori is a great source of iodine too.

1 cup rice of choice: short-grain is ideal

1 tablespoon rice vinegar

4 nori sheets

SUSHI FILLERS

Avocado

Omelette, thinly sliced into strips

Pan-fried tempeh, thinly sliced into strips

Tinned tuna

Carrot and cucumber

Start by rinsing your rice in a sieve until the water runs clear.

Cook the rice according to the packet instructions in a pot, rice cooker or pressure cooker.

Once cooked, stir through the rice vinegar.

Lay a piece of nori on a board, shiny side down.

Spread the rice out covering the whole sheet – don't forget the sides. Press it down with a spoon or your fingers to make sure it's as flat as possible. Leave some room with no rice at the top edge.

Place your fillings approximately 3 cm (1¼ in) from the bottom of the sheet (one-third of the way up).

Start by rolling your sushi where the filling begins, upwards, holding the filling in place.

To help it stick, slightly wet the edge at the end to stick down well.

With a sharp knife, cut into 1 cm (½ in) pieces.

SWAPSIES

You can swap the rice for quinoa.

STORAGE

Store in the fridge for 2 days.

AGE
12 months +

SERVES
4 people

PREP TIME
5 minutes

COOK TIME
35 minutes

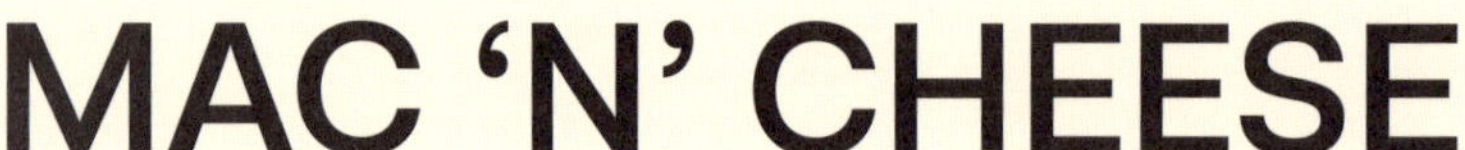

MAC ‘N’ CHEESE

- ½ small cauliflower, cut into florets
- ½ zucchini (courgette), roughly chopped
- 3 cups macaroni (or pulse pasta)
- 1 tablespoon butter
- 3 tablespoons spelt flour
- 1½ cups milk of choice
- 1 cup grated cheddar cheese
- 1 teaspoon garlic powder
- 1 teaspoon onion powder
- ¼ teaspoon pepper
- a handful of breadcrumbs

OPTIONAL ADD-INS:

- ½ cup cherry tomatoes, quartered
- 420 g (15 oz) tinned tuna

This creamy mac ‘n’ cheese recipe, filled to the brim with cauliflower and zucchini (courgette), is a family-friendly twist on a classic. Top it off with an extra layer of cheddar cheese for the perfect crispy finishing touch.

Preheat the oven to 180°C (360°F).

Bring a large saucepan of water to the boil.

Steam the cauliflower and zucchini until soft then drain and let the veggies cool.

Meanwhile, cook the pasta as per packet instructions. Drain, rinse with cold water and set aside to cool while making the sauce.

In a separate saucepan, melt the butter, whisk in the flour and slowly whisk in the milk, half a cup at a time, ensuring there are no lumps. Keep whisking until the mixture thickens and starts to bubble, this can take up to 10 minutes.

Then, stir in ½ cup of the cheese and the garlic powder and onion powder. Whisk for another minute or two until well-combined. Season with pepper, if desired.

Add the sauce, cauliflower and zucchini to a blender. Blitz until smooth and creamy.

Pour the cooled pasta into a large baking dish. If you’d like to add in tomatoes and/or tuna, do that now.

Pour the sauce over the pasta, give it a good mix and top with the remaining cheese and sprinkle the breadcrumbs on top.

Place in the oven and cook for 15–20 minutes or until golden and crispy on top.

SWAPSIES

For a gluten-free version, swap the wheat pasta for pulse pasta, swap the spelt flour for buckwheat flour or gluten-free oat flour.

STORAGE

Store in the fridge for up to 3 days. To freeze this dish, assemble, cool and skip the baking step. Store in the freezer for up to 3 months. When ready to serve, thaw and bake in the oven as per the method.

SERVES
1

PREP TIME
5–10 minutes

COOK TIME
5 minutes

AGE
12 months +

QUESADILLAS

This is a quick meal that ticks all the boxes: it's rich in iron, balanced, nutritious and delicious. The strategic cut allows you to fold the wrap into the perfect pocket, which means less mess and a meal that's easier for your little one to handle. This healthy wrap brings the same delicious, Mexican-inspired flavours we love to the table while packing in the nutritional goodness.

1 wrap of choice or one of our Quinoa wraps (page 263)

1 tablespoon extra-virgin olive oil

COMBO IDEAS

Mighty veggie bolognese (page 218), cheddar cheese and avocado

Hummus, shredded chicken and sliced tomato

Tinned black beans, cheddar cheese and avocado

Tinned salmon, avocado and corn

Secret sauce (page 209), cheddar cheese and onion

Spinach, mozzarella and olives

Cut the wrap down the middle with a pair of kitchen scissors, stopping halfway so that you're left with four quadrants.

Arrange your chosen fillings in each of the four quadrants of the wrap. Use 2 tablespoons of filling per quadrant. Our favourite combination is our Mighty veggie bolognese (page 218), cheddar cheese and double avocado.

Starting from the bottom-left corner, fold one section up then across and, finally, down to create a square pocket.

Heat the oil in a frying pan over a medium–low heat. Place the filled wrap in the pan and cook until it becomes golden brown and crispy. This usually takes about 2 minutes. Flip it over and cook for another 2 minutes on the other side.

TO SERVE

Cut the wrap into halves or quarters and serve with a dollop of yoghurt and Guacamole (page 255).

SWAPSIES

Pick any topping you like but ensure there are at least one to two binders such as cheese, avocado, hummus or our Secret sauce (page 209).

STORAGE

These are best enjoyed warm, straight from the pan.

AGE
9 months +

SERVES
Makes 12 balls

PREP TIME
15 minutes

COOK TIME
25 minutes

CHEESY BROCCOLI BOMBS

FOR THE FILLING

1 small head of broccoli, chopped into florets

½ cup peas

¾ cup mozzarella cheese, grated

¼ cup cooked quinoa

1 egg

½ teaspoon garlic powder

½ teaspoon ground cumin

½ teaspoon paprika

Crack of black pepper

FOR THE COATING:

2 pieces stale bread

1 egg, whisked

extra-virgin olive oil, for drizzling

TO SERVE

Serve with aioli or yoghurt for dipping.

Broccoli finally gets the hero moment it deserves in these healthy cheesy balls. These flavour bombs are packed with greens and quinoa and loaded with goodness. Bite into the crispy exterior and savour the creamy centre, all the while knowing you're nourishing your little one with every delicious bite.

Preheat the oven to 200°C (390°F)

Steam the chopped broccoli for 4 minutes, and 2 minutes before it's finished, add your peas to steam together.

Meanwhile, add the stale bread to a food processor and blitz to fine breadcrumbs.

Add all the filling ingredients to a bowl and mash with a fork, making sure everything is mixed together well.

Roll the mixture into twelve balls.

To a bowl, add the whisked egg. To another bowl, add your breadcrumbs.

Dip each ball into the egg, followed by the breadcrumbs.

Drizzle a little extra-virgin olive oil over the balls and transfer to a baking tray. Bake for 20–30 minutes, or until crispy and golden, turning them halfway through so they evenly brown on both sides.

SWAPSIES

You can use ½ cup premade breadcrumbs instead of making your own.

Swap mozzarella for cheddar cheese.

Quinoa can be swapped for rice.

STORAGE

Store in the fridge for up to 3 days in an airtight container or in the freezer for up to 3 months.

SERVES
Makes 20

PREP TIME
20 minutes

COOK TIME
20–25 minutes

AGE
12 months +

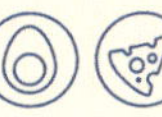    

LITTLE VEGGIE SAUSAGE ROLLS

Nothing says party food like a yummy tray of sausage rolls! These flavoursome 'sausage' rolls are a great way to get veggies and legumes into your little one's belly. They're packed with veggies and are perfect for lunchboxes or parties.

FOR THE FILLING

- 2 garlic cloves, peeled
- ½ brown onion, roughly chopped
- ½ cup brown mushrooms, roughly chopped
- 1 small carrot, roughly chopped
- ½ cup capsicum (bell pepper), roughly chopped
- 400 g (14 oz) brown lentils, rinsed and drained
- 1 egg
- 1 tablespoon tomato paste (concentrated purée)
- ½ cup grated cheddar cheese
- 1 teaspoon dried thyme

FOR THE PASTRY

- 2 sheets puff pastry
- 1 egg, whisked
- 1 tablespoon sesame seeds or poppy seeds for topping (optional)

Preheat the oven to 200°C (390°F) and line a baking tray with baking paper.

Add the garlic, onion, mushrooms, carrot and capsicum to a food processor and blend until finely chopped. Next, add the drained lentils, egg, tomato paste, cheese and thyme and blend for a few seconds until well combined. You want the mixture to have some texture so don't overblend it.

Cut each square sheet of puff pastry into three long rectangles. Add the mixture down the middle of each long rectangle and use your hands to shape it tightly together into a long sausage shape.

Brush a little egg along the long end and roll the pastry over the filling, sealing the ends by gently pressing them together.

Fold each side of the pastry up to meet in the middle then press the sides together to cover the filling. Using a pastry brush, brush some of the egg along the pastry to 'stick' it together.

Cut the rolls into bite-sized pieces, approximately ten for each sheet.

Brush with egg. You can also sprinkle sesame seeds or poppy seeds over them at this point.

Transfer to the baking tray lined with baking paper and bake for 20–25 minutes or until golden.

SWAPSIES

Use whatever veggies you have in the fridge! Spinach, broccoli and cauliflower would all work well.

We use a wholemeal spelt butter puff pastry, but any puff pastry would work.

STORAGE

Store in the fridge for up to 3 days in an airtight container or in the freezer for up to 3 months.

MAINS

AGE
6 months +

SERVES
4

PREP TIME
15 minutes

COOK TIME
1 hour 15 minutes (depending on the size of your chicken)

ROAST CHOOK

- 1.5–2 kg (3 lb 5 oz–4 lb 6 oz) whole chicken
- 4 cups veggies of choice: sweet potatoes, potatoes, broccoli, carrots, pumpkin (squash) and zucchini (courgette)
- ½ cup chicken stock or broth
- 1 brown onion, halved
- 2 tablespoons ghee, melted
- 2 tablespoons finely chopped fresh parsley
- 2 garlic cloves, minced
- 1 tablespoon lemon juice, reserve the lemon for stuffing the chook
- 2 tablespoons extra-virgin olive oil

TO SERVE

Serve with a side of steamed greens, doused in butter or extra-virgin olive oil.

FIRST FOOD

Offer the veggies in finger-sized pieces. You can serve a chicken drumstick, removing the skin, loose gristle and small bones or offer soft pieces of shredded chicken. Alternatively, make a purée using juices from the pan to thin out the chicken and veggies.

This is a simple yet nourishing recipe that makes enough for leftovers the next day. The chook is tender, juicy and packed with flavour – and did we mention it's a one-pan dish? Winner winner, chicken dinner!

Preheat the oven to 200°C (390°F).

Chop up the veggies and place them in the bottom of a large roasting pan. Pour the stock or broth over the veggies then add the halved onion to the middle of the pan.

In a bowl, mix together the melted ghee, parsley, garlic and the lemon juice.

Rub half of the mixture under the skin of the chicken and the remainder on top of the chicken skin. Stick the reserved lemon into the cavity and place the chicken on top of the onion in the middle of the roasting pan.

Drizzle the extra-virgin olive oil over the chicken and veggies and season, if desired.

Cook for 15 minutes then turn the oven down to 180°C (360°F) and cook for another hour or so until the chicken juices run clear.

SWAPSIES

For a dairy-free version, swap the ghee for extra-virgin olive oil.

STORAGE

Store in the fridge for up to 3 days.

SERVES
6

PREP TIME
10 minutes

COOK TIME
20–30 minutes

AGE
6 months +

SECRET SAUCE

This is a pasta sauce glow up specially crafted with little ones in mind. Bursting with vibrant roast veggies and a creamy taste and punch of protein from the tofu, it's great for pasta, on rice or quinoa and even works as a delicious pizza sauce.

½ brown onion, roughly chopped
1 garlic clove, roughly chopped
1 carrot, roughly chopped
½ sweet potato, roughly chopped
1 cup cauliflower, roughly chopped
1 red capsicum (bell pepper), roughly chopped
½ teaspoon dried basil
extra-virgin olive oil, for drizzling
150 g (5½ oz) organic silken tofu, drained
400 g (14 oz) tinned tomatoes

Preheat the oven to 180°C (360°F).

To a baking dish, add the onion, garlic, chopped veggies, dried basil and a good drizzle of extra-virgin olive oil. Mix until well combined. Place in the oven and roast for 20–30 minutes, or until the veggies are cooked until soft.

Add cooked vegetables to a food processor with the tofu and tinned tomatoes and blend until smooth and creamy.

TO SERVE

Serve with pasta, quinoa, rice, in wraps or even as a pizza sauce!

SWAPSIES

For a soy-free version, swap the tofu for 425 g (15 oz) tin of cannellini beans.

You can use whatever veggies you've got in the fridge.

STORAGE

Store in the fridge for up to 6 days in an airtight container or in the freezer for 3 months

AGE
9 months +

SERVES
4

PREP TIME
10 minutes

COOK TIME
20 minutes

  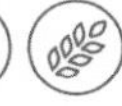

ZESTY PESTO PASTA

- 1 cup Zesty pesto (page 271)
- 400 g (14 oz) chicken breasts, skin off
- 300 g (10½ oz) pasta of choice
- ½ cup pasta water

Prepare to meet the superhero dish that steals the show in our households! Brace yourself for a blend of oh-so-many fresh herbs, tender pasta and shredded chicken. It's a great mid-week meal that will leave your tastebuds cheering.

Fill a saucepan with enough water to cover the chicken breasts and bring to the boil. Once the water has reached boiling point, add the chicken, **cover** and turn off the heat immediately. Leave the chicken to poach for 20 minutes.

Bring a saucepan of water to the boil and cook pasta according to the packet instructions. Conserve ½ a cup of the pasta water and put aside. Drain and set aside.

Shred the chicken with a fork.

Once the pesto, pasta and chicken are ready, mix them together in a large bowl with the reserved pasta water until well combined.

SWAPSIES

For a wheat-free version, swap the wheat pasta for pulse pasta.

For a vegetarian version, swap the chicken for firm tofu.

STORAGE

Store in the fridge for up to 3 days in an airtight container.

SERVES
6–8

PREP TIME
10 minutes

COOK TIME
2–3 hours

AGE
6 months +

CHICKEN SOUP

Chicken soup is truly good for the soul. There is nothing more nourishing and wholesome than a bowl of this chicken and vegetable goodness. This soup has anti-inflammatory properties, is full of prebiotic vegetables and the long cooking time draws out the collagen-rich gelatin from the chicken bones.

- 2 tablespoons extra-virgin olive oil
- 4 garlic cloves, minced
- 1 brown onion, diced
- ¼ leek, finely chopped
- 1 teaspoon fresh ginger, minced
- 2 celery stalks, roughly chopped
- 2 carrots, diced
- 1.5 kg (3 lb 5 oz–4 lb 6 oz) whole chicken or a mix of 4 chicken thighs and 4 drumsticks
- 2 litres (68 fl oz) chicken stock or Hug-in-a-cup broth (page 279)
- 1 teaspoon apple-cider vinegar
- 1 cup raw barley
- ½ cup fresh parsley, chopped
- Squeeze of lemon juice

Heat the oil in a large saucepan over a medium–high heat.

Sauté the garlic, onion, leek and ginger until they become translucent.

Add the celery and carrot and stir for 3–5 minutes. Then add the whole chicken, the stock and the apple-cider vinegar and bring to the boil.

Once the soup has come to boil, turn the heat down to a simmer, place the lid on and cook for 1 hour.

At the 1-hour mark, add the barley and the parsley, and continue cooking for another hour.

After another hour, remove the chicken and debone then add the chicken meat back into the pot and stir. Season, if desired, and finish with a squeeze of lemon juice.

SWAPSIES

Twenty minutes before the soup is finished cooking you could also add some frozen peas and spinach/silverbeet (Swiss chard).

If gluten sensitive, swap barley for brown rice.

Instead of using a whole chicken, you could do a combination of chicken thighs, wings, drumsticks and breast.

Instead of cooking the soup in a saucepan, you could also put everything in a slow cooker and cook on low for 6 hours.

STORAGE

Store in the fridge for up to 4 days in an airtight container or in the freezer for up to 3 months.

FIRST FOOD

Offer the broth in a sippy cup and the chicken and vegetables as finger foods. Alternatively, purée the soup to a liquid consistency. Swap out barley for brown rice to omit gluten before allergen exposure. Aim for a lower sodium stock or swap for bone broth.

AGE
9 months +

SERVES
4

PREP TIME
10 minutes

COOK TIME
8 minutes

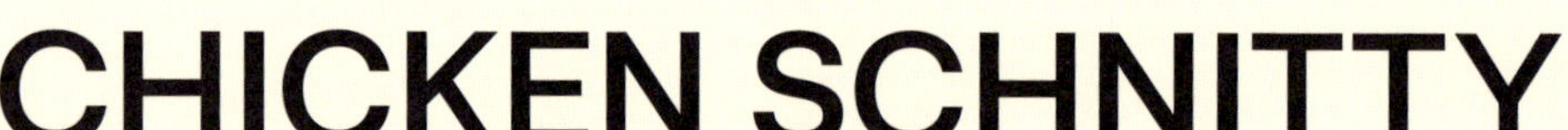

CHICKEN SCHNITTY

- 1 cup sourdough breadcrumbs or 1 large piece of day-old sourdough bread
- ¼ teaspoon lemon zest
- ½ teaspoon garlic powder
- ½ teaspoon paprika
- 1 egg, whisked
- 3 tablespoons arrowroot flour
- 400 g (14 oz) chicken breasts or tenderloins
- 1 tablespoon extra-virgin olive oil or ghee

TO SERVE

Serve with roast veggie chips, a side of Secret sauce (page 209) for dipping and lemon wedges.

Tender on the inside, crunchy on the outside, our wholesome chicken nugget upgrade is easy to whip up and even the tiny food critics will come back for more.

Add the stale bread to a food processor and blitz to fine breadcrumbs.

To a shallow bowl, add the breadcrumbs and stir in the lemon zest, garlic powder and paprika.

To another shallow bowl, add the whisked egg.

Lastly, sprinkle the arrowroot flour on a plate.

Slice the chicken breasts lengthways into two thinner halves, or use tenderloins.

Dredge the chicken in the flour, then dip it in the egg on both sides and then coat it in the breadcrumb mixture. Ensure both sides are thoroughly coated.

Heat the extra-virgin olive oil in a frying pan over a medium–high heat.

Add the chicken to the pan and cook on each side for a few minutes until golden. Cooking time will depend on the size of your chicken pieces. Check it's completely cooked through before serving.

SWAPSIES

Swap the arrowroot flour for oat flour or whole-wheat flour.

Swap the chicken for another protein of choice such as fish, tempeh or tofu.

You can omit the seasonings from the crumb.

STORAGE

Best served warm out of the pan.

SERVES
6

PREP TIME
30 minutes

COOK TIME
50 minutes

AGE
7 months +

NO-PASTA LASAGNE

This hearty dish is a favourite in our homes. It's packed with iron, loaded with veggies and the cheeses make it rich in calcium.

- 1 large sweet potato, thinly sliced lengthways
- 3 zucchinis (courgettes), thinly sliced lengthways
- 2 tablespoons extra-virgin olive oil, plus extra for coating
- 500 g (1 lb 2 oz) grass-fed minced (ground) beef
- 1 brown onion, diced
- 3 garlic cloves, minced
- 680 ml (23 fl oz) tomato passata (puréed tomatoes)
- 1 teaspoon dried basil
- 1 teaspoon dried oregano
- ½ cup spinach (fresh or frozen)
- 250 g (9 oz) ricotta
- 1 egg
- Handful chopped basil
- ¼ cup parmesan cheese

Preheat the oven to 180°C (360°F).

Coat the sweet potato and zucchini in extra-virgin olive oil then place them on a baking tray lined with baking paper and bake for 20 minutes or until soft.

Meanwhile, in a deep frying pan over a medium–high heat, add 1 tablespoon extra-virgin olive oil and fry off the onion and garlic until translucent. Add your mince and stir until brown.

Stir in the the passata and dried herbs. Once the sauce starts to bubble, turn down the heat to low and leave the sauce to simmer for 20–30 minutes.

A few minutes before removing the pan from the heat, stir in your spinach.

While the sauce is simmering, make the ricotta filling by stirring an egg through the ricotta in a bowl. If the mixture feels too thick, pour in up to ¼ cup water. It should be a nice spreadable consistency.

In a deep baking dish, start compiling your lasagne layers. Add 1 tablespoon of extra-virgin olive oil to the bottom of the dish then add half the sweet potato slices covering the base of the dish.

Add ⅓ cup of the mince covering all of the sweet potato and sprinkle with basil. Next, add half of the zucchini slices followed by another ⅓ cup of the mince and half of the ricotta mix. Sprinkle some more basil leaves on top. Add the rest of the sweet potato, the remaining mince and the remaining zucchini slices.

Finish with the remaining ricotta, spreading it out as much as possible and sprinkle parmesan cheese over the top of the lasagne to finish.

Bake in the oven for 20 minutes or until the lasagne is nice and golden on top.

SWAPSIES

Eggplant (aubergine) is also a great veggie to use alongside the zucchini and sweet potato.

You can use our Mighty veggie bolognese (page 218) as the mince filling to pack in extra veggies.

Parmesan cheese is optional for babies under 12 months.

STORAGE

Store in the fridge for up to 3 days or in the freezer for up to 3 months.

AGE
6 months +

SERVES
8

PREP TIME
10 minutes

COOK TIME
45 minutes

MIGHTY VEGGIE BOLOGNESE

- 3 garlic cloves, minced
- 1 brown onion, diced
- 1 cup mushrooms, roughly chopped
- 1 cup broccoli, roughly chopped
- 1 zucchini (courgette), roughly chopped
- 1 carrot, roughly chopped
- 2 celery stalks, roughly chopped
- 1 tablespoon extra-virgin olive oil
- 500 g (1 lb 2 oz) grass-fed organic minced (ground) beef
- 2 tablespoons tomato paste (concetrated purée)
- 680 ml (23 fl oz) tomato passata (puréed tomatoes)
- ½ teaspoon dried thyme
- ½ teaspoon dried parsley
- ½ teaspoon dried basil
- ½ teaspoon dried oregano
- ½ teaspoon coconut/raw/brown sugar

TO SERVE

With pasta of choice, in a Quesadilla (page 199) or on Pizza (page 242).

Our spin on a family classic has three cups of veggies that are blended up so they will go undetected by even the fussiest of eaters. And the best part is you can freeze any leftovers for those moments when you need a quick iron-rich meal up your sleeve.

Blitz the garlic, onion, mushrooms, broccoli, zucchini, carrot and celery in a food processor until finely chopped.

Add the extra-virgin olive oil to a large saucepan over a high heat.

Add the blended veggies to the saucepan and sauté for about 5 minutes, stirring regularly, then add the mince and stir until brown.

Next, stir in the tomato paste, passata and the herbs. Place the lid on the saucepan, turn the heat down to medium and let the sauce simmer for 30–45 minutes, stirring every 15 minutes or so. Season, if desired.

A few minutes before removing from the heat, add in the sugar to remove any acidic flavour.

STORAGE

Store in the fridge for up to 3 days in an airtight container or in the freezer for up to 5 months.

FIRST FOOD

Offer as a purée thinned with breastmilk, formula or bone broth. Alternatively, smear onto finger foods or use as a dip.

SERVES
4

PREP TIME
5 minutes

COOK TIME
20 minutes

AGE
6 months +

MEAN GREEN PASTA

This creamy, cheesy pasta sauce is packed with beautiful greens and prebiotic-rich ingredients. It's a simple way to get some veggies into a pasta sauce and the subtle combination of zesty lemon and ricotta elevates the dish. Say goodbye to the veggie battles and hello to your new favourite pasta.

300 g (10½ oz) pasta of choice

1 tablespoon extra-virgin olive oil

2 garlic cloves, minced

½ leek, roughly chopped

1 head of broccoli, roughly chopped

½ zucchini (courgette), roughly chopped

½ cup peas

¾ cup pasta water

zest of 1 lemon

125 g (4½ oz) ricotta

Cook the pasta according to the packet instructions then drain, making sure to reserve ¾ cup of pasta water.

Heat the oil in a saucepan over a medium heat.

Sauté the garlic and leek until translucent. Add the broccoli and zucchini to the pan and sauté for 5–10 minutes until it softens then add the peas and sauté for a further 5 minutes.

To a food processor, add the sautéed vegetables, pasta water, lemon zest and ricotta and blend until smooth and creamy.

Mix the sauce through the pasta and season, if desired.

SWAPSIES

For a dairy-free version, swap the ricotta for ½ cup chopped avocado.

For a wheat-free version, swap the wheat pasta for pulse pasta.

STORAGE

Store the pasta and sauce in the fridge for up to 5 days or store the sauce in the freezer for up to 3 months.

AGE
7 months +

SERVES
4

PREP TIME
10 minutes

COOK TIME
20 minutes

THE MED PASTA

- 1 tablespoon extra-virgin olive oil
- 4 garlic cloves, minced
- 4 cups cherry tomatoes, chopped
- 3 tablespoons kalamata olives, pits removed and finely chopped
- 2 tablespoons fresh parsley, finely chopped
- 250 g (9 oz) tinned mackerel or tuna, drained
- 300 g (10½ oz) pasta of choice
- ⅓ cup reserved pasta water
- ¼ teaspoon salt

TO SERVE

Top with Parmesan cheese and a generous squeeze of lemon. Add chilli flakes for the adults.

This quick and easy Mediterranean-inspired dish is super versatile. You can use tinned mackerel or tuna straight from the pantry – either way it's a great way to get oily fish into your family's diet and introduce your little ones to big flavours!

Add the oil to a large frying pan over a medium–high heat. Add the garlic and sauté for a minute or two.

Meanwhile, cook the pasta according to the packet instructions then drain, making sure to reserve ⅓ cup of pasta water.

Add your chopped tomatoes to the frying pan and fry them off for a minute then turn down the heat to a simmer for approximately 5 minutes.

Once the tomatoes have started to soften, stir in a few tablespoons of the pasta water at a time. This will help slowly thicken the sauce. Repeat another three times every few minutes. Once all the water has been stirred in and the tomato sauce is thick, stir in the olives, parsley and your fish of choice. Then toss the cooked pasta into the pan. Season, if desired.

SWAPSIES

For a fish-free version, swap the mackerel or tuna for cooked prawns (shrimp).

We love to use a wholegrain pasta or for a wheat-free option choose a pulse pasta for pulse or lentil pasta.

Omit olives under 12 months.

STORAGE

Store in the fridge for up to 3 days.

SERVES
6

PREP TIME
15 minutes

COOK TIME
30 minutes

AGE
6 months +

HEARTY LENTIL SOUP

This hearty, comforting soup is one we've been making on repeat for years. It's thick enough to be a soup your little one can eat on their own and can be puréed to serve as a first food. This is one of our favourite ways to get iron and fibre-rich lentils into your little one's diet.

- 1 cup dried lentils (pre-soaked for a minimum of 2 hours)
- 1 tablespoon extra-virgin olive oil
- 3 garlic cloves, minced
- 1 brown onion, finely chopped
- ¼ leek, finely chopped
- 1 zucchini (courgette), finely chopped
- 1 carrot, finely chopped
- 1 small sweet potato, finely chopped
- 400 g (14 oz) tinned tomatoes
- 1.5 litres (51 fl oz) bone broth or stock
- ½ teaspoon dried thyme

Start by soaking your lentils (see soaking instructions on page 79).

Heat the oil in a saucepan over a high heat then sauté the garlic, onion and leek. Cook until the vegetables are translucent.

Add the zucchini, carrot and sweet potato, stirring for another 5 minutes.

Pour in the tinned tomatoes, lentils, broth and thyme. Reduce to a medium heat and let the soup cook for 30 minutes, stirring intermittently.

Blend half of the soup with a hand-held blender (or in a blender). Leave the rest of the soup as is. This makes the finished soup super creamy and is an important step for perfecting the overall texture.

FIRST FOOD

Offer as a purée, thinning with breastmilk, formula or bone broth if needed. Alternatively, smear onto finger foods or use as a dip.

SWAPSIES

All types of lentil work well in this soup.

If you don't have time to soak the lentils, you can use tinned lentils and reduce the stock or water to 750 ml (25 fl oz).

For a vegan version, swap the bone broth for vegetable broth or vegan stock.

If you don't have dried thyme, oregano will work too.

STORAGE

Store in the fridge for up to 5 days or in the freezer for up to 3 months.

AGE
9 months +

SERVES
6

PREP TIME
10 minutes

COOK TIME
40 minutes

CREAMY COCONUT FISH CURRY

- 1 tablespoon coconut oil
- 1 teaspoon cumin seeds
- 1 onion, diced
- 2 garlic cloves, finely chopped
- 1 teaspoon fresh ginger, grated
- 1 teaspoon ground turmeric
- ½ teaspoon ground cumin
- ½ teaspoon paprika
- 2 tablespoons tomato paste (concentrated purée)
- 400 g (14 oz) tinned tomatoes
- 400 ml (13½ fl oz) coconut milk
- 425 g (15 oz) tin chickpeas, drained and rinsed
- 2 zucchinis (courgettes), roughly chopped
- 1 head of broccoli, roughly chopped
- 1 cup frozen peas
- 500 g (1 lb 2 oz) white fish of choice, cut into strips

TO SERVE

Pair with quinoa or rice and add a dollop of your yoghurt of choice on top.

The richness of the sauce in our simple take on a creamy fish curry is balanced by the mix of vibrant veggies and chickpeas. This is a great dish for introducing your little one to a medley of spices and big flavours!

Heat the coconut oil in a large saucepan over a medium–high heat. Add the cumin seeds and let them cook for 1–2 minutes until they start to pop. Add the onion, garlic and ginger to the pan and sauté for or a few minutes until they become translucent.

Add the spices and the tomato paste and stir well until the onions are evenly coated then pour in the tinned tomatoes and coconut milk and stir until well combined.

Place the lid on, turn down the heat to medium and let the sauce simmer for 20 minutes or until it starts to thicken.

Add in the vegetables and chickpeas and stir for another 10 minutes or until they start to soften.

Gently place the fish in, stirring to coat the fish with the sauce. Put the lid back on and let the curry simmer for another 10 minutes until the fish is cooked through.

SWAPSIES

Any veggies you have on hand will work here – cauliflower, capsicum (bell pepper) and pumpkin (squash) are some of our faves.

STORAGE

Store in the fridge for up to 3 days or in the freezer for up 3 months.

SERVES
4

PREP TIME
5 minutes

COOK TIME
20 minutes

AGE
9 months +

 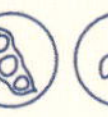   

QUINOA RAINBOW RICE

Our wholesome take on fried rice is filled with lots of goodness but doesn't compromise on flavour. It's an all-in-one balanced dish, rich in choline and protein from the eggs, a great variety of vegetables to support growing guts and a slow-burning carb, quinoa, to keep little tummies nice and full.

Start by cooking your quinoa as per the packet instructions.

While the quinoa is cooking, whisk the eggs in a small bowl then scramble them in a frying pan over a medium heat before transferring them to a clean bowl and setting aside.

In the same pan as you cooked the eggs, heat 1 tablespoon of the sesame oil and sauté the onion, garlic, spring onion and ginger until soft.

Add the rest of the chopped veggies and sauté for 10 minutes, stirring occasionally.

Finally, add the cooked quinoa, the scrambled egg, the tamari and another tablespoon of sesame oil. Stir well then remove from the heat.

2 cups cooked quinoa
4 eggs
2 tablespoons sesame oil
½ onion, finely diced
3 garlic cloves, minced
1 small bunch of spring onions (scallions), chopped
1½ teaspoons grated ginger
3 cups of veggies, finely chopped: carrots, zucchini (courgette), corn, broccoli, peas, edamame
1½ tablespoons tamari or soy sauce
1 tablespoon sesame seeds
Squeeze of lemon or lime juice

TO SERVE

Sprinkle the rice with sesame seeds and a squeeze of lemon or lime juice.

SWAPSIES

Rice can be used instead of quinoa.

For a sesame-free version, omit the sesame seeds and swap the sesame oil for coconut oil.

STORAGE

Store in the fridge for up to 3 days.

AGE
12 months +

SERVES
6

PREP TIME
15 minutes

COOK TIME
20 minutes

GREEN FRITTATA

- 1 tablespoon extra-virgin olive oil
- ½ brown onion, diced
- 2 garlic cloves, minced
- 1 cup broccoli, finely chopped
- ½ cup frozen or fresh spinach
- ½ cup frozen peas
- 6 eggs
- 1 teaspoon dried oregano
- 3 tablespoons of cottage cheese
- ½ cup grated cheddar cheese

Elevate your meal prep game with this yummy green frittata: a versatile dish that adds both flavour and nutrition to your weekly meals. Packed with protein and abundant in choline, this frittata not only provides a satisfying and nourishing option but also ensures you're getting your fair share of greens. Whip up this simple dish in advance, slice it up and enjoy it as a standalone meal or a lunchbox addition throughout the week.

Preheat the oven to 180°C (360°F).

Heat the oil in a frying pan over a medium–high heat. Sauté the onion and garlic until translucent.

Sauté the broccoli for a few minutes or until it starts to soften. Add the spinach and peas and sauté for another few minutes.

In a large bowl, whisk the eggs, oregano and cottage cheese together. Pour in the veggie mix along with ¼ cup of the cheddar cheese and stir well to combine.

Transfer the mixture to your baking dish of choice, sprinkle the remaining cheddar cheese on top.

Bake for 15–20 minutes or until cooked through and golden.

SWAPSIES

Most veggies will work here. Ensure you choose vegetables with similar cooking time to the broccoli so it's all cooked through well together. Capsicum (bell pepper), silverbeet (Swiss chard) and mushrooms are delicious in a frittata.

STORAGE

Store in the fridge for up to 4 days in an airtight container or in the freezer for up to 3 months. If freezing, place slices between pieces of baking paper to avoid sticking.

SERVES
6

PREP TIME
15 minutes

COOK TIME
30 minutes with canned lentils, 45 minutes with dried lentils

AGE
6 months +

  #1

VEGGIE LENTIL CURRY

Our veggie-packed lentil curry is a perfect choice for busy weeknights. The garlic, ginger and turmeric have antioxidant and anti-inflammatory properties, the lentils have a hearty dose of protein, which will keep everyone satisfied for longer, and the coconut milk is full of healthy fats. If you or your little one prefers a milder flavour, simply top with a dollop of yoghurt.

1 tablespoon coconut oil

1 onion, finely chopped

3 garlic cloves, minced

½ tablespoon fresh ginger, minced

2 teaspoons curry powder

1 teaspoon ground turmeric

Pinch of cracked black pepper

5 cups vegetables, finely chopped (we use zucchini/courgette, carrot, broccoli, cauliflower and peas)

425 g (15 oz) tinned brown lentils or 1 cup dried lentils (add 3 cups water or stock to absorb)

400 ml (13½ fl oz) coconut milk

400 g (14 oz) tinned chopped tomatoes

Handful of coriander (cilantro) leaves

Heat the coconut oil in a large saucepan over medium-high heat. Sauté the onion for a couple of minutes then add the garlic and ginger. Once fragrant, add the curry powder, turmeric and pepper and stir well.

Place all the veggies in the pan and cook for 5 minutes. Once the veggies start to lightly fry, add in the lentils, coconut milk and tinned tomatoes and let the curry simmer for 15–20 minutes with the lid on. If using dried lentils, adjust the cooking time to 30 minutes until soft.

STORAGE

Store in the fridge for up to 3 days or in the freezer for up to 3 months.

TO SERVE

Spoon over rice or pasta with a dollop of your yoghurt of choice and some coriander on top.

FIRST FOOD

Offer as a purée, thinning with breastmilk, formula or bone broth, if needed. Alternatively, smear onto finger foods or use as a dip.

AGE
6 months +

SERVES
Makes
16 meatballs

PREP TIME
20 minutes

COOK TIME
30 minutes

MEATBALLS AND VEGGIE SAUCE

FOR THE SAUCE

- 1 tablespoon extra-virgin olive oil
- 1 onion, diced
- 2 garlic cloves, roughly chopped
- 1 carrot, finely chopped
- ½ head of broccoli, roughly chopped
- 1 large zucchini (courgette), roughly chopped
- 1 teaspoon dried basil
- 680 ml (23 fl oz) tomato passata (puréed tomatoes)
- 2 tablespoons tomato paste (concentrated purée)

FOR THE MEATBALLS

Follow our Burger recipe on page 241.

TO SERVE

Spoon over your pasta of choice and top with parmesan cheese.

With five different veggies packed into this meatball sauce, it's a dish you are going to feel excited to serve up to the family! Blending the veggies is the best way to pack in all that goodness and flavour while creating a smooth traditional-style sauce. Serve with our veggie-infused, iron-rich meatballs and you have a winning combo everyone will love.

Alternatively use this sauce as a tomato sauce for pasta to get those veggies into your little one's pasta dishes.

Heat the oil in a frying pan over a medium heat. Sauté the onion and garlic until they become translucent.

Add the carrot, broccoli and zucchini and stir for 5 minutes until the veggies start to soften.

Set the pan aside and blend the veggies in a food processor with the basil, tomato passata and tomato paste, until smooth.

Make the meatball mixture according to our instructions for Burger patties (see page 241).

Roll the mixture into small balls, you'll need approximately 2 tablespoons per ball, and place them on a plate.

Heat up the frying pan again and fry off the meatballs until they're browned but not cooked through.

Pour in the veggie sauce and leave the meatballs to finish cooking. This will take about 10–12 minutes.

STORAGE

Store in the fridge for up to 3 days or in the freezer for up to 3 months.

SERVES
6

PREP TIME
10 minutes

COOK TIME
3 hours 50 minutes

AGE
6 months +

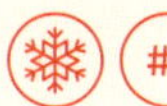

SLOW-COOKED LAMB

The low and slow method we use for our lamb ensures that the meat is moist and falls off the bone. YUM! This recipe is a fantastic way to get iron into your little one's diet. Its tender texture and delicious taste make it a great first food, too. Beyond its iron content, lamb is also a source of zinc, protein and oozes with vitamins and minerals.

- 1.5–1.8 kg (3.3–4 lbs) lamb shoulder
- 5 garlic cloves, halved lengthways
- 4 sprigs fresh rosemary, cut into approximately 3 cm (1¼ in) pieces
- 1 carrot, roughly chopped
- 3 potatoes, quartered
- 1 brown onion, quartered
- 375 ml (12 fl oz) bone broth or stock
- 3 tablespoons extra-virgin olive oil
- 1 head of broccoli, roughly chopped

Preheat the oven to 150°C (300°F).

Place the lamb shoulder in an ovenproof dish and pierce the top and sides with a knife, making ten holes deep enough to stuff the garlic cloves into. Fill the holes with garlic and the rosemary sprigs.

Arrange the carrot, potatoes and onion around the lamb and pour over the broth or stock.

Rub the extra-virgin olive oil into the lamb and over the veggies. Season, if desired.

Cover with foil and roast for 3½ hours.

Remove the lamb from the oven and baste it with the broth from the dish. At this point, add the broccoli. Turn the oven up to 200°C* (390°F) and place the dish back in uncovered for 20 minutes.

Remove the lamb from the oven and let it rest for 20 minutes before serving. Carve using a sharp knife to loosen the thick skin. The meat should fall off the bone.

*Keep an eye on your lamb, ensuring it doesn't burn. Some ovens are stronger and may need to be lowered to 180°C (360°F).

FIRST FOOD

Offer root vegetables as soft stick-shaped pieces. Shredded lamb can also be offered as long as it passes the squish test. Alternatively, purée with extra juices from the pan to thin.

SWAPSIES

You can use most veggies here: we also like sweet potatoes, pumpkin (squash), capsicum (bell pepper) and zucchini (courgette).

STORAGE

Store in the fridge for up to 3 days or in the freezer for up to 3 months.

AGE
6 months +

SERVES
6

PREP TIME
10 minutes

COOK TIME
30 minutes

BEANIE NACHOS

2 tablespoons extra-virgin olive oil

1 sweet potato, peeled and roughly chopped

1 zucchini (courgette), roughly chopped

1 onion, diced

½ head of garlic, trimmed

1 teaspoon dried basil

345 ml (11½ fl oz) tomato passata (puréed tomatoes)

425 g (15 oz) tin kidney beans, drained and rinsed

200 g (7 oz) corn chips

½ cup grated cheddar cheese

TO SERVE

Guacamole (page 255), cherry tomatoes, squeeze of lime, coriander (cilantro) and yoghurt.

FIRST FOOD

Omit corn chips and cheese. Offer as a purée, thinning with breastmilk, formula or bone broth if needed. Alternatively, smear onto finger foods or use as a dip.

Our take on nachos is a crowd pleaser. This recipe is jam-packed with veggies, protein and iron-rich kidney beans. From the crunchy corn chips to the gooey melted cheese, every bite is sure to please. Topped with creamy avocado and zesty salsa, it is a fun dinner option or party dish that all ages will enjoy!

Preheat the oven to 200°C (390°F).

In a small bowl, coat the sweet potato, zucchini, onion and garlic with extra-virgin olive oil and dried basil then transfer to a baking tray lined with baking paper.

Bake for 20 minutes or until the veggies are soft and cooked through.

Add the roasted veggies back into the bowl and mash them well with a fork.

Add the passata and kidney beans to the bowl and stir to combine.

To assemble the nachos, spread the corn chips out on a baking tray lined with baking paper and cover with the bean mix. Top with grated cheese and bake for 10–15 minutes until the chips are nice and crispy and the cheese is gooey and bubbling.

SWAPSIES

You could swap out the corn chips for homemade roasted sweet potato slices.

STORAGE

Store the nacho sauce in the fridge for up to 5 days or in the freezer for up to 3 months.

SERVES
10 patties

PREP TIME
15 minutes

COOK TIME
30 minutes

AGE
6 months +

BURGER AND CHIPPIES

Carrots and onion are incorporated into these mouth-watering burger patties, ensuring that every bite is packed with wholesome goodness and making them extra moist and tender. Layer with your favourite burger toppings and serve with our crunchy sweet potato chippies and you have a winning combo! Plus, these burger patties can also be rolled into small balls to make meatballs for our Meatballs and veggie sauce (page 234) or into koftas for a first food!

FOR THE CHIPPIES

- 2 large sweet potatoes
- 2 tablespoons extra-virgin olive oil
- ½ teaspoon onion powder
- ½ teaspoon garlic powder

FOR THE BURGER PATTIES

- 500 g (1 lb 2 oz) minced (ground) beef or lamb
- 2 garlic cloves, finely chopped
- ½ brown onion, grated
- 1 egg
- 1 carrot finely grated
- ½ teaspoon ground cumin
- 1 teaspoon paprika
- 3 tablespoons spelt flour
- 1 tablespoon extra-virgin olive oil (for frying)

BURGER TOPPINGS

- Cheese
- Sliced tomatoes
- Lettuce
- Fried onions
- Avocado
- Beetroot (beet)
- Pickles
- Burger buns

Preheat the oven to 200°C (390°F).

Cut the sweet potatoes into 1 cm (½ in) sticks. Put them in a bowl with the oil and the spices and toss to combine.

Spread them out on a baking tray lined with baking paper.

Bake for 15 minutes until they're slightly brown and crispy on the bottom, then flip and cook until the other side is crispy. This will take about 10 minutes.

Meanwhile, start making the burger patties. Add all the ingredients, except the oil, to a large bowl and mix with your hands until evenly combined. Season, if desired.

Heat the oil in a frying pan over a medium-high heat or fire up your barbecue. Roll the mixture into ten balls and shape each portion into a patty with your hands, approximately 2 cm (¾ in) thickness.

Cook the patties for about 4 minutes on each side, or until browned and cooked through.

STORAGE

Store leftovers in the fridge for up to 2 days. To freeze patties, wrap cooked patties individually and then store them in a freezer bag. They will keep in the freezer for up to 2 months. Defrost overnight in the fridge before reheating. The patties can also be frozen raw.

To cook, make sure the patties are fully defrosted then heat them through in a frying pan (on low) or in the oven for 10–15 minutes.

AGE
9 months +

SERVES
Makes 4 small pizza bases

PREP TIME
10 minutes

COOK TIME
30 minutes

PIZZA

FOR THE BASE

Yoghurt flatbread (page 256)

SAUCE IDEAS

1: Secret sauce (page 209)

2: Zesty pesto (page 271)

3: Tomato paste (concentrated purée) or passata (puréed tomatoes)

CHEESE IDEAS

1: Grated cheddar cheese

2: Sliced fresh mozzarella

3: Goat's cheese

TOPPINGS IDEAS

1: Mighty veggie bolognese (page 218)

2: Sliced baked chicken with sliced zucchini (courgette) and onions

3: Sliced mushrooms and olives

A great alternative to takeaway pizza, our version is not only the healthiest, but also the most delicious pizza that everyone in the family will be gobbling up. The base is packed with protein, there are no additives or preservatives to worry about and the toppings are full of nutrients. Get your little one involved in making the pizza and enjoy this meal family style.

Preheat the oven to 180°C (360°F), or preheat a barbecue.

Make your yoghurt flatbread as per the instructions on page 256.

Spread your sauce over the uncooked pizza base, followed by cheese and toppings of choice. Get your little one involved: let them choose their favourite toppings and help you layer them on the pizza.

Place in the oven and cook until the pizza is golden and the cheese is bubbly. This will take about 10 minutes.

STORAGE

Store the cooked pizza in the fridge for up to 2 days or freeze before cooking for up to 2 months.

SERVES
4

PREP TIME
10 minutes

COOK TIME
30 minutes

AGE
7 months +

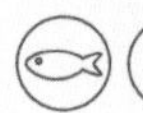

RAINBOW FISH BAKE

This fuss-free meal is our go-to for busy weeknights or lazy weekends. It's well balanced and only uses one tray so cleaning up is minimal – a winner in itself!

- 1 cup wholemeal couscous
- 1 teaspoon stock powder
- 1½ cups of boiling water
- 1 zucchini (courgette), halved and thinly sliced
- 1 cup cherry tomatoes, halved
- ½ head of broccoli, chopped
- ¼ cup kalamata olives, pitted
- 3 tablespoons extra-virgin olive oil
- 4 × 100 g (3½ oz) fish fillets (ling or barramundi work well)
- 1 teaspoon garlic powder
- 1 teaspoon dried oregano
- ½ sliced red onion

Preheat the oven to 180°C (360°F). To a deep ovenproof dish, add your couscous, stock and boiling water and stir to combine.

Add your chopped vegetables on top, coated in approximately 2 tablespoons of the extra-virgin olive oil and bake for 15 minutes.

Remove the tray from the oven and stir the cooked veggies through the couscous.

Add the fish and olives, drizzle with the remaining oil and sprinkle on the garlic powder and oregano. Cook for another 15 minutes until the fish is cooked through.

SWAPSIES

Most veggies can be used here – we also like capsicum (bell pepper), eggplant (aubergine) and pumpkin (squash). However, make sure they're all cut into similar-sized pieces to ensure an even cooking time.

For babies under 12 months, omit olives.

STORAGE

Store in the fridge for up to 2 days in an airtight container.

AGE
9 months +

SERVES
6

PREP TIME
10 minutes

COOK TIME
30 minutes

  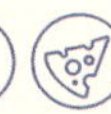  

VEGGIE-PACKED SHEPHERD'S PIE

FOR THE TOPPING

2 cups cauliflower, cut into large florets
2 large potatoes, diced
2 tablespoons butter
⅓ cup milk of choice
2 tablespoons breadcrumbs
2 tablespoons grated cheese

FOR THE FILLING

1 tablespoon extra-virgin olive oil
3 garlic cloves, minced
1 onion, finely chopped
1 carrot, finely diced (or grated for babies under 12 months)
2 tablespoons tomato paste (concentrated purée)
850 g (30 oz) canned lentils
120 ml (4 fl oz) vegetable stock
400 g (14 oz) tinned tomatoes
1 teaspoon dried thyme
1 teaspoon dried rosemary
1 cup frozen peas
1 tablespoon tamari or soy sauce

This hearty dish is a great way to get lentils into your little one's diet. It's also a beautiful vegetarian alternative to traditional Shepherd's pie and a budget-friendly meal.

To prepare the topping, add the potatoes and cauliflower to a large pot of boiling water. Cook for 10 minutes or until you can pierce a fork through the potatoes. Drain and add veggies to a large bowl.

Mash potato and cauliflower and mix through the butter and milk. Alternatively, add all the topping ingredients into a blender and blend until smooth.

Heat the oil in a large frying pan over a medium heat then sauté the garlic and onion until they become translucent.

Add the carrot and cook for 3–5 minutes, stirring occasionally.

Add the lentils, stock, tinned tomatoes, tomato paste, thyme, rosemary, peas and tamari. Stir to combine and let it simmer for 10 minutes. Season, if desired.

Once the filling has started simmering, preheat the oven to 200°C (390°F).

Add the pie filling to an ovenproof dish and spread the topping over the filling, making sure to cover the filling entirely.

Sprinkle breadcrumbs and grated cheese on top of the pie before brushing with some extra-virgin olive oil.

Grill for 10 minutes or until the topping is golden.

SWAPSIES

For a dairy-free version, swap butter for extra-virgin olive oil and swap the cheese for 1½ tablespoons of nutritional yeast.

You can use dried lentils instead of canned. Combine 1 cup dried brown lentils with 3 cups stock and simmer for 30 minutes.

STORAGE

Store in the fridge for up to 3 days or in the freezer for up to 3 months.

SIDES AND CONDIMENTS

50 VEGGIE SIDEKICKS

1. Roasted broccoli topped with cheddar or parmesan cheese*.
2. Sweet potato chips cooked in coconut oil with cinnamon.
3. Medley of oven chippies: potato, beetroot (beet) and sweet potato cooked in extra-virgin olive oil and a sprinkle of sea salt.
4. Sweet potato mash with rosemary and garlic.
5. Roasted zucchini (courgette) chips doused in ghee* and onion powder.
6. Store-bought boiled beetroot with extra-virgin olive oil, feta* and crushed walnuts*.
7. Roasted potato medallions doused in butter* and garlic.
8. Smashed potatoes with extra-virgin olive oil, rosemary and a sprinkle of sea salt.
9. Tinned chickpeas with cumin.
10. Green beans pan-fried in ghee* with garlic and crushed hazelnuts*.
11. Raw vegetable salad: sliced cherry tomatoes, cucumber, carrots and olives.
12. Avocado sprinkled with hemp seeds or ground linseed (flax seed).
13. Sauerkraut
14. Baked sweet potato wedges in extra-virgin olive oil seasoned with paprika and cumin.
15. Corn on the cob doused in butter* and a squeeze of lime.
16. Steamed peas and/or corn with butter*.
17. Kale chips baked in extra-virgin olive oil and a sprinkle of sea salt.
18. Pumpkin (squash) wedges with extra-virgin olive oil, cumin and pepper.
19. Steamed cauliflower topped with grated cheese* or butter*.
20. Edamame beans*
21. Olives
22. Pickles
23. Brussel sprouts pan-fried in extra-virgin olive oil, topped with sesame seeds* with a mustard dip.
24. Celery with nut butter*.

25. Shredded cabbage and carrot mixed with mayonnaise.
26. Cucumbers sticks with extra-virgin olive oil and dill.
27. Steamed veggies with yoghurt* to dip.
28. Asparagus cooked in extra-virgin olive oil and sprinkled with sesame seeds*.
29. Oven-roasted carrots tossed with honey and thyme.
30. Baked cauliflower with extra-virgin olive oil, turmeric and pepper.
31. Caprese salad: tomatoes, mozzarella*, basil and extra-virgin olive oil.
32. Pan-fried mushrooms in butter*, garlic and rosemary.
33. Mashed cauliflower topped with parsley and parmesan cheese*.
34. Black beans, tomato, corn, avocado, red onion, coriander (cilantro) and lime salad.
35. Baked potato stuffed with cheese* and tomato.
36. Pickled veggies
37. Raw zucchini (courgette) ribbons with extra-virgin olive oil and dill.
38. Sliced capsicum (bell pepper) with yoghurt dip.
39. Mixed frozen veggies stirred through pulse pasta.
40. Lettuce boats with tomato, corn and pickles.
41. Cucumber sticks with hummus.
42. Roasted beetroot (beet) sticks cooked in ghee* with slivered almonds and squeeze of lemon.
43. Sautéed and shredded brussel sprouts with lemon and ricotta*.
44. Quick guacamole with tomato and coriander and seasoned with cumin and lime.
45. Cauliflower grated as rice and cooked in sesame oil* with garlic.
46. Grilled eggplant (aubergine) drizzled with tahini*.
47. Spinach sautéed in butter* and garlic.
48. Stir-fried mixed vegetables with tamari* and ginger.
49. Baked butternut squash cubes seasoned with cinnamon and nutmeg.
50. Sautéed zucchini (courgette) noodles with cherry tomatoes and basil.

**Indicates top allergen*

AGE
12 months +

SERVES
4

PREP TIME
5 minutes

COOK TIME
20 minutes

CRISPY RAINBOW CHIPPIES

1 raw beetroot (beet)
1 large sweet potato
2 tablespoons extra-virgin olive oil

TO SERVE

We love these with a Chicken schnitty (page 214) for a healthy take on a classic pub meal. Serve with guacamole (page 255) or Zesty pesto (page 271).

We all love chippies so we've given the everyday chip a healthier twist. The potatoes are subbed out for beetroot (beet) and sweet potatoes to make sure your little one gets a boost of colour and antioxidants in their diet. These can be enjoyed as a snack or alongside a meal.

Preheat the oven to 180°C (360°F).

With a mandolin or a knife, thinly slice the beetroot and potato into 'potato chips', aiming for slices as thin as possible.

Lay out the slices evenly on a baking tray lined with baking paper, drizzle with extra-virgin olive oil and a touch of sea salt.

Bake for 20 minutes, turning halfway through, or until they are golden and crisp.

SWAPSIES

These chippies can be made with any root vegetable, such as parsnip or potato.

STORAGE

These don't usually last long in our houses! Best eaten warm out of the oven.

Chips
SERVES
4

PREP TIME
5 minutes

COOK TIME
10 minutes

Guac
SERVES
4

PREP TIME
10 minutes

AGE
12 months +

CHIPS 'N' GUAC

Indulge in a classic and irresistible combination with our pita chips and guacamole recipe. The crispy, golden pita chips serve as the perfect vehicle for our take on guacamole. This is a great snack and sure to be a hit at any party.

FOR THE PITA CHIPS

3 large wholemeal pita breads

2 tablespoons extra-virgin olive oil

¼ teaspoon garlic powder

FOR THE GUAC

2 ripe avocados

2 tablespoons lime juice

½ teaspoon garlic powder

¼ teaspoon ground cumin

1 tablespoon finely chopped coriander (cilantro)

2 tablespoons finely chopped red onion (optional)

1 finely chopped roma (plum) tomato

PITA CHIPS

Preheat the oven to 200°C (390°F).

With scissors or a knife, cut your pita breads into triangles.

Either brush the pita with extra-virgin olive oil or if you don't have a brush, add them to a bowl with extra-virgin olive oil then season with garlic powder, mixing with your hands until all the pita is well coated.

Add the pita to a baking tray lined with baking paper, making sure the triangles are not on top of one another, and bake for 10 minutes, or until golden and crisp.

GUAC

Cut the avocados in half, remove the stones and score the inside of the avocado with a knife. Scoop out the flesh into a bowl and mash with a fork.

Add the lime juice and all the spices and mix well. Add the remaining ingredients and mix until combined.

STORAGE

Store chips in an airtight container at room temperature for up to a week. The guac is best enjoyed fresh.

AGE
9 months +

SERVES
Makes 4 flatbreads

PREP TIME
30 minutes

COOK TIME
Approximately
4 minutes per piece

YOGHURT FLATBREADS

1¼ cups spelt flour
½ teaspoon baking powder
¼ teaspoon salt
¾ cup Greek yoghurt
Coconut oil, for frying

TO SERVE

Top the flatbread with some butter and sprinkle with freshly chopped parsley.

These flatbreads are easy and healthy, and with just four ingredients, they're a great way to get your little one involved in the kitchen. Flatbreads are the perfect side to a meal and a huge hit with the whole family. We love using these as a base for homemade pizzas, as wraps or for dipping into curries.

Sift the flour, baking powder and salt into a mixing bowl and stir to combine.

Add the yoghurt and mix until well combined.

Let the dough sit for 20 minutes on your benchtop.

Divide it into four pieces.

Sprinkle some additional flour on your bench and start kneading a piece into the flour, then roll it out with a rolling pin or your hands. Repeat this step with the remaining dough.

If the dough is too sticky, slowly sprinkle more flour until you achieve a dough consistency.

Heat some coconut oil in a frying pan over medium heat. Place a flatbread in the pan and cook on each side for 2–4 minutes or until golden.

SWAPSIES

Spelt flour can be swapped with any flour of choice. If you use self-raising flour, you won't need the baking powder.

STORAGE

Wrap the flatbreads in foil and keep them at room temperature for up to 3 days or in the freezer for up to 1 month in an airtight container

SERVES
Makes 4 wraps

PREP TIME
5 minutes

COOK TIME
20 minutes

AGE
6 months +

OAT WRAPS

Our oat wraps are the easiest, most affordable and healthiest wraps you will ever serve up. Supermarket wraps can be filled with so many additives so we've devised a quick and simple alternative. Oats are high in fibre, they are slow carbohydrates and they will fill your little one's belly for longer. Add their favourite fillings and enjoy!

Coconut oil, for frying
1 cup rolled oats
1 cup water

Heat a frying pan over a medium heat and lightly grease with coconut oil.

To a blender, add the oats and water and blend until smooth. Season with salt (optional).

Pour 2 tablespoons of the batter into the pan, moving it around to create a small circular shape. For a larger wrap, use ¼ cup.

Once it starts to bubble, flip the wrap and cook it on the other side for 2–3 minutes, or until lightly golden.

TO SERVE

Some of our favourite fillings include: avocado, cheese, tuna, tinned salmon or our Berry good jam (page 275).

STORAGE

Layer wraps between baking paper to avoid them sticking together. Store in the fridge for up to 3 days.

AGE
12 months +

SERVES
4

PREP TIME
5 minutes

COOK TIME
20–25 minutes

SWEET 'N' STICKY CARROTS

1½ tablespoons extra-virgin olive oil, melted butter or ghee

2 teaspoons honey*

¼ teaspoon ground cinnamon

4 carrots, quartered lengthways

**Omit honey for babies under 12 months.*

TO SERVE

Pairs well with Pink hummus (page 272).

Our honey-roasted carrots are a yummy update to the humble carrot. Coated in a simple honey glaze and roasted to perfection, these carrots will have your little one asking for seconds. Carrots can be fun after all!

Preheat the oven to 200°C (390°F).

In a bowl, stir together the extra-virgin olive oil, honey and cinnamon. Add your chopped carrots and mix until they're well coated.

Lay the carrots on a baking tray lined with baking paper: the more they are separated, the more they will crisp up.

Bake for 20–25 minutes until the carrots are golden and soft.

SWAPSIES

Honey can be swapped for maple syrup.

STORAGE

Store in the fridge for up to 3 days.

SERVES
Makes 8 wraps

PREP TIME
3 hours
(soaking time)

COOK TIME
40 minutes

AGE
6 months +

QUINOA WRAPS

These wraps are made with a quinoa base so they're high in protein and amino acids. They're also a good gluten- and wheat-free alternative to traditional wraps. The malleability allows the wraps to easily encase your favourite fillings, transforming them into a convenient and delicious option for quick lunches, or as a side to a main meal.

FOR THE WRAP

1 cup uncooked quinoa

coconut oil or extra-virgin olive oil, for frying

1 cup filtered water or Hug-in-a-cup broth (page 279)

OPTIONAL ADD-INS

1 tablespoon broth concentrate if using water

⅛ teaspoon ground turmeric

With a crack of pepper

TO SERVE

Add your favourite fillings, dip the wraps in soup or serve as a side dish with a curry.

Rinse the quinoa in a sieve then add it to a bowl and cover with cold water. Leave to soak overnight (or for a minimum of 3 hours).

Melt the coconut oil or extra-virgin olive oil in a frying pan over a medium heat. Smear the oil with paper towel to help evenly distribute it.

Drain the quinoa and add it to a food processor with the filtered water, plus any optional add-ins, and blitz on high until the batter is a smooth and runny consistency.

Pour ¼ cup of batter (or ⅛ cup for mini wraps) into the pan, swirling to ensure the batter coats the pan evenly for a nice even wrap.

Cook for 2–3 minutes then flip with a spatula and cook the other side. Once both sides are cooked, leave to cool on a wire rack.

Make sure to avoid stacking your wraps until they've cooled or they'll stick together.

SWAPSIES

For a vegan version, omit the broth or swap it for a vegetable broth.

STORAGE

Layer wraps between baking paper to avoid them sticking together. Store in the fridge for up to 5 days in an airtight container.

AGE
9 months +

SERVES
Makes ½ cup

PREP TIME
2 minutes

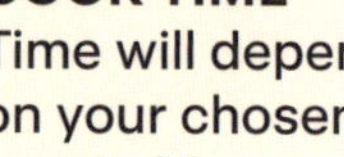

COOK TIME
Time will depend on your chosen vegetable or protein.

BABLE CRUMB

FOR THE CRUMB

¼ cup hemp seeds

¼ cup LSA or ground linseed (flax seed)

½ teaspoon garlic powder

¼ teaspoon finely grated lemon rind (optional)

1 tablespoon extra-virgin olive oil or ghee

FOR THE EGG WASH

1 egg, whisked

FOR THE FLOUR BASE

¼ cup arrowroot, besan (chickpea flour) or oat flour

Sometimes we like to crumb our little one's food to make things just a bit more exciting and, well, crunchy! Unfortunately, store-bought breadcrumbs can be filled with so many unnecessary additives making a DIY crumb is a much healthier option! Use this crumb to coat zucchini (courgette) sticks, fish, chicken and even tofu – it works every time.

To a shallow bowl, add all the crumb ingredients, except the oil, and mix until well combined.

To another shallow bowl, add your whisked egg.

Lastly, to another shallow bowl, add your flour.

Begin by dredging your chosen protein or veggie in the flour, coating both sides. Next, dip into the egg wash, coating on both sides, followed by the crumb mixture. Make sure all pieces are well coated.

Heat the oil in a frying pan over a medium–high heat.

Add to the pan and cook on each side for a few minutes until golden. (Cooking time will depend on the protein or veggie). Always check if it's cooked through before serving. If the crumb is burning, lower the heat to ensure the protein or vegetable is cooked properly.

Alternatively, you can bake in the oven at 180°C (360°F) on a baking tray lined with baking paper.

STORAGE

Store crumb in an airtight container in the fridge for up to a week.

SERVES
Makes 1 cup

PREP TIME
10 minutes

COOK TIME
10 minutes

AGE
6 months +

SEED BUTTER

Finally, a spread that has maximum lunchbox appeal! Try our allergen-friendly and nutritious seed butter, packed with protein, fibre, antioxidants, vitamins and minerals. This creamy and delicious spread will keep your little one satisfied and nourished throughout the day.

2 cups mixed sunflower seeds and pepitas (pumpkin seed)

¼ teaspoon sea salt*

½ tablespoon maple syrup*

* Omit maple syrup and salt for babies under 12 months.

Preheat the oven to 180°C (360°F).

Spread out the seeds on a baking tray lined with baking paper. Bake for 10–15 minutes until they're nice and golden.

Blitz the seeds, sea salt and maple syrup in a food processor until a paste starts to form. This could take anywhere from 4–10 minutes depending on your machine. Make sure you are scraping down the sides every few minutes. Blend until a buttery smooth consistency forms.

STORAGE

Store in the fridge for up to 3 weeks.

AGE
12 months +

SERVES
Makes ⅓ cup

PREP TIME
5 minutes

DATE PASTE

8 medjool dates
½ cup boiling water

Date paste* is a great swap for refined sugar when baking delicious goodies. Dates are naturally sweet and filled with fibre, antioxidants and an abundance of other key minerals.

Add your dates to a small bowl and cover them with boiling water. Leave the dates to soften for 5 minutes.

Remove the dates from the water (reserve the water) and remove the pits.

Add the dates to a blender with ½ cup of the date water.

Blitz until well combined and a nice paste consistency forms.

STORAGE

When using date paste in recipes, store any remaining date paste for up to a month or in the freezer for up to 3 months.

**Date paste can be used instead of granulated sugar as a 1:1 ratio and a 1.5:1 ratio when replacing with a liquid sugar such as maple syrup or honey (1.5 parts date paste:1 part honey).*

SERVES
Makes 1 cup

PREP TIME
10 minutes

AGE
6 months +

ZESTY PESTO

Our homemade pesto is fresh, full of nutrients and will excite your little one's tastebuds. It's also so quick and easy to whip up – serve it on toast, in a sandwich or mixed through pasta.

- 1 cup steamed broccoli
- 2 tablespoons walnuts
- 2 tablespoons sunflower seeds
- ½ cup fresh basil leaves
- ½ cup fresh parsley leaves
- 2 large garlic cloves
- ⅓ cup extra-virgin olive oil
- 2 tablespoons lemon juice
- ¼ cup grated parmesan cheese

Start by steaming your broccoli. While its steaming, toast your walnuts and sunflower seeds in a frying pan until they begin to pop and turn golden. This should take a couple of minutes.

Add all the ingredients to a food processor and blend until well combined.

SWAPSIES

For a dairy-free option, swap the parmesan cheese for nutritional yeast.

STORAGE

Store in the fridge for up to 5 days in an airtight container or in the freezer for up to 3 months.

AGE
7 months +

SERVES
Makes 1½ cups

PREP TIME
5 minutes

PINK HUMMUS

- 400 g (14 oz) tin chickpeas, drained and rinsed
- 250 g (9 oz) pre-cooked beetroot (beet)
- 1 garlic clove, peeled
- ¼ cup tahini
- ¼ cup extra-virgin olive oil
- ¼ cup lemon juice
- 1 teaspoon ground cumin

Add a vibrant twist to traditional hummus with our beetroot (beet) hummus recipe. This colourful variation will capture your little one's attention and it's bursting with antioxidants from the beetroot.

Add all the ingredients to a blender and blitz until well combined.

STORAGE

Store in the fridge for up to a week or in the freezer for up to 4 months.

SERVES
Makes 1 cup

COOK TIME
10 minutes

AGE
6 months +

BERRY GOOD JAM

This jam has been a staple in our fridges ever since our kids started solids. It's incredibly versatile and is delicious served on toast, in sandwiches, with yoghurt, in oats, in a smoothie or even on its own. Packed with omega-3s and fibre from the chia seeds and antioxidants from the berries, it's a great alternative to sugary store-bought jams.

2 cups frozen or fresh berries of choice
¼ cup chia seeds
½ cup boiling water

In a small saucepan over a low heat, combine all the ingredients and cook for 10 minutes, stirring constantly. Mash the berries with a fork, making sure none are kept whole.

SWAPSIES

Strawberries, blueberries or raspberries work well here, or a mix.

You could add ¼ teaspoon of vanilla extract or 1 teaspoon of honey for babies over 12 months.

STORAGE

Store in the fridge for up to 7 days or in the freezer for up to 3 months.

FIRST FOOD

Offer as a purée, thinning with breastmilk or formula if needed. Alternatively, smear onto finger foods such as poached pear or use as a dip.

AGE
24 months +

SERVES
Makes 2 cups

PREP TIME
10 minutes

CHOCCY SPREAD

1¾ cups raw hazelnuts
¼ cup raw cacao powder
¼ cup coconut sugar
1 tablespoon coconut oil
¼ teaspoon sea salt

Here's our healthier take on a childhood favourite. An additive-free alternative to supermarket spreads, our version is also bursting with antioxidants. Spread it generously on toast, in a sandwich for a delightful and wholesome snack, or offer it on the side of some fruit as a delicious dip.

Preheat the oven to 180°C (360°F).

Spread out the hazelnuts on a baking tray and bake for 10 minutes until they start to become golden.

Rub the hazelnuts gently in a tea towel (dish towel) to remove the skins.

To a food processor, add all the ingredients and blend for 5 minutes. Every processor is different, so continue blending until a smooth, buttery texture forms.

If you need more liquid, add another tablespoon of coconut oil to create a creamier consistency.

STORAGE

Store in an airtight jar at room temperature for up to a month.

SERVES
Makes 2.5 litres (85 fl oz/10 cups)

PREP TIME
10 minutes

COOK TIME
5 hours

AGE
6 months +

HUG-IN-A-CUP BROTH

Bone broth is called *liquid gold for* a reason. Oozing with gelatinous collagen from the chicken bones, this staple recipe is the perfect addition to yours and your little one's meals. Add it to soups, purées, stews, curries, freeze in ice blocks, add it when cooking rice and quinoa, or offer it to your little one in a sippy cup. The health benefits of bone broth go beyond its protein and collagen content – it supports digestion, our gut lining, holds anti-inflammatory properties and is shown to support brain function.

1 brown onion, halved
2 garlic cloves
1 carrot, halved
2 celery stalks, trimmed
2 tablespoons apple-cider vinegar
600 g (1 lb 5 oz) chicken feet
275 g (10 oz) chicken necks
2 chicken carcasses

To a large saucepan over a medium–high heat, add all the ingredients and cover with just enough water to cover the bones. Filtered cold water is best (not boiling water).

Once the water reaches a simmer, turn the heat down to low and cook for a minimum of 5 hours with the lid off. This can keep cooking for as long as you like, but 5–7 hours is ideal. Top up the water as necessary.

Strain the broth into a large bowl. You can discard the chicken bones or keep them for a second batch of broth.

Transfer the broth to airtight containers or jars.

SWAPSIES

For a beef broth, swap the chicken for beef bones.

STORAGE

Store in the fridge for up to 5 days or in the freezer in an ice-cube tray or airtight container for up to 3 months.

SWEETS

AGE
24 months +

SERVES
Makes 6 brownies

PREP TIME
10 minutes

COOK TIME
25 minutes

BEANIE BROWNIE BITES

- 400 g (14 oz) tin black beans, drained and rinsed
- ¼ cup coconut oil
- ¼ cup raw cacao powder
- ¼ cup maple syrup
- ½ cup rolled oats
- ½ teaspoon vanilla extract
- ½ teaspoon baking powder
- 2 tablespoons chocolate chips

Our beanie brownie bites are fudgy, delicious and surprisingly nutritious! Packed with protein and fibre from the black beans, they're everything we love in a brownie recipe, plus more! These good-for-you brownie bites are great for dessert or on a party platter.

Preheat the oven to 180°C (360°F).

Add all the ingredients, except the chocolate chips, to a food processor and blend until well combined.

Mix through the chocolate chips.

Grease a muffin tray or mini muffin moulds, and pour in the batter.

Bake for 20–25 minutes.

Let the brownies cool for 10 minutes then transfer to a wire rack for another 10 minutes to cool completely.

STORAGE

Store in the fridge for up to 5 days or in the freezer for up to 3 months. If freezing, separate the brownies in between layers of baking paper.

SERVES
Makes 10 bites

PREP TIME
5 minutes

COOK TIME
20 minutes

AGE
18 months +

BLONDIE BITES

These irresistible chickpea blondies are the ultimate high-protein and wholesome snack. They're a delightful way to incorporate chickpeas into your little one's diet. Naturally sweet, with a soft and chewy texture, these blondies will be loved at first bite.

- 400 g (14 oz) tin chickpeas, drained and rinsed
- ½ cup smooth peanut butter
- ¼ cup maple syrup
- ½ teaspoon baking powder
- ¼ cup chocolate chips (optional)

Preheat the oven to 180°C (360°F) and line a loaf (bar) tin with baking paper.

Add all the ingredients, except the chocolate chips, to a food processor and blend until smooth.

Stir in half the chocolate chips, transfer the mixture into the loaf tin and sprinkle with the remaining chips.

Bake for 20–25 minutes or until golden.

Let the blondies cool for 10 minutes then transfer to a wire rack for another 10 minutes to cool completely. Cut the blondies into squares to serve.

SWAPSIES

Chocolate chips can be swapped out for berries or chopped up dates.

STORAGE

Store in the fridge for up to a week in an airtight container or in the freezer for up to 3 months.

AGE
24 months +

SERVES
Makes 12 crackles

PREP TIME
5 minutes

COOL TIME
1 hour

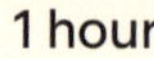

CHOCCY CRACKLES

- ½ cup melted coconut oil
- 2 tablespoons honey*
- 2 tablespoons raw cacao powder
- 2 cups puffed wholegrain rice
- ¼ cup hemp seeds

**Omit honey for babies under 12 months.*

This is a healthy take on one of our childhood favourites. These crackles have minimal sugar, maximum flavour and are a crowd pleaser. They're filled with hemp seeds, an excellent source of both omega-3s and healthy fats, and raw cacao powder, which has antioxidants and gives the crackles that naturally chocolatey flavour.

Mix the melted coconut oil, honey and raw cacao powder together in a bowl until well combined.

Add the puffed wholegrain rice and hemp seeds and stir to combine.

Pour the mixture into a silicone muffin mould, or if you don't have silicone moulds, use baking paper to line a muffin tin. Press down firmly on the crackles and leave to set in the freezer for at least an hour or until the crackles are firm.

SWAPSIES

Puffed rice can be replaced with puffed quinoa for a higher-protein snack. Honey can be swapped for maple syrup.

STORAGE

Store in the freezer for up to 3 months.

SERVES
Makes 12 cookies

PREP TIME
5 minutes

COOK TIME
15 minutes

AGE
18 months +

CHEWY COOKIES

Packed with healthy fats, these cookies are both delicious and nutritious. Quick and easy to make, they are the perfect cookie to make with your little ones. With a soft and chewy texture and a hint of almond flavour, these cookies are sure to be a hit with kids and adults alike.

¼ cup extra-virgin olive oil
3 tablespoons maple syrup
1 teaspoon baking powder
1 cup almond meal
1 cup rolled oats
3 tablespoons grass-fed collagen powder (optional)
4 medjool dates, pitted and finely chopped

Preheat the oven to 180°C (360°F) and line a baking tray with baking paper.

Mix the extra-virgin olive oil and maple syrup together in a bowl then add all the other ingredients.

With damp hands, roll the cookies into balls, place them on the baking tray, then flatten them with a fork or press down with your hands.

Bake for 15 minutes.

Let cool for 10 minutes before transferring the cookies to a wire rack to cool completely.

SWAPSIES

Dates can be swapped out for 3 tablespoons chocolate chips.

STORAGE

Store at room temperature in an airtight container for up to 5 days.

AGE
18 months +

SERVES
Makes 12 cookies

PREP TIME
15 minutes

COOK TIME
12 minutes

FESTIVE COOKIES

- 1 egg
- 2 tablespoons melted coconut oil
- ¼ cup maple syrup
- 1 teaspoon vanilla extract
- 2 cups almond meal
- ½ cup besan (chickpea flour)
- ½ teaspoon bicarbonate of soda (baking soda)
- ¼ teaspoon ground cinnamon
- ⅛ teaspoon ground nutmeg
- Chocolate chips (optional)

These cookies are perfect for any special occasion. The combination of almond meal and besan (chickpea flour) gives them a beautifully nutty and earthy flavour while providing a boost of protein and fibre. The cinnamon and nutmeg give these cookies a warm and cosy aroma that fills the air. Get your little one involved with stamping out fun shapes and decorating the cookies with chocolate chips or raisins.

Preheat the oven to 180°C (360°F) and line a large baking tray with baking paper.

In a large mixing bowl, stir together the wet ingredients until well combined, then add the dry ingredients and give the mixture a good mix.

Roll the dough into a big ball and place it in between two sheets of baking paper.

With a rolling pin or the side of a glass, roll the dough out to a 1 cm (½ in) thickness.

Take your festive cookie cutters of choice and cut out as many shapes as you can. You can roll up any leftover batter and repeat the process a second time.

Decorate the tops with chocolate chips. Transfer to lined baking tray and bake for 12 minutes, checking at the 8-minute point until the tops are nicely golden.

Leave the cookies to cool on the tray for 10 minutes before transferring to a wire rack to cool completely.

SWAPSIES

Besan (chickpea flour) can be swapped for any flour of choice.

If you don't have cookie cutters, simply roll these into balls and press down with a fork to make circular cookies. They will need slightly more time to cook so keep an eye on them to ensure they don't burn.

STORAGE

Store at room temperature for up to 5 days in an airtight container or freeze for up to 3 months.

SERVES
Up to 16 slices

PREP TIME
20 minutes

COOK TIME
20 minutes

AGE
12 months +

 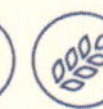  

BABLE BIRTHDAY CAKE

This carrot cake is a showstopping dessert that will make any celebration extra special. It was a huge success at our two toddlers' combined 2nd birthday party and was enjoyed by children and adults alike!

Preheat the oven to 180°C (360°F).

Line the bottom and sides of two 23 cm (9 in) round cake tins with baking paper. (If you only have one cake tin, cook the cakes one at a time.)

Grate the carrots then squeeze out as much excess liquid as you can with your hands or into a tea towel (dish towel).

In a large mixing bowl, whisk the eggs then add the melted coconut oil, maple syrup and vanilla and mix until well combined.

Mix in the grated carrot.

In a separate bowl mix up all the dry ingredients.

Fold the dry ingredients through the wet ingredients until combined.

Divide the cake batter equally between the two prepared cake tins. Place both cakes in the oven and bake for 20 minutes or until the tops have browned. The cakes are cooked when a knife inserted in the middle of the cakes comes out clean.

Let the cakes cool for 10 minutes in the tins before carefully transferring them to a wire rack and letting them cool completely.

Mix all your icing ingredients together in a large mixing bowl until all the bubbles and lumps are gone.

Pour half the icing on top of one cake and use a butter knife or spatula to spread evenly to the edge of the cake.

Place the second cake on top of the first cake. Ice the top, leaving a bit of a gap uniced around the edges.

STORAGE

Best stored in the fridge for up to 5 days.

The cakes can be frozen for up to 3 months without the frosting. If freezing, use sheets of baking paper in between each cake to avoid them sticking.

FOR THE CAKE
(MAKES TWO LAYERS)

- 450 g (1 lb) carrots, peeled
- 4 eggs
- ⅔ cup melted coconut oil
- ½ cup maple syrup
- 1 teaspoon vanilla extract
- ½ cup coconut sugar
- 1½ cups spelt flour
- 2 cups almond meal
- 2 teaspoons baking powder
- 1 teaspoon bicarbonate of soda (baking soda)
- 1 teaspoon ground cinnamon
- ¼ teaspoon ground nutmeg
- ¼ teaspoon ground ginger

FOR THE ICING

- 500 g (1 lb 2 oz) cream cheese, at room temperature
- ½ cup Greek yoghurt
- ¼ cup maple syrup
- 2 teaspoons vanilla extract
- 2 teaspoons grated lemon zest

TOPPINGS

- ¼ cup walnuts, finely chopped
- 1 teaspoon grated lemon zest

TO SERVE

Top with chopped walnuts, lemon zest and slices of figs (or any other fruit of choice).

AGE
12 months +

SERVES
4

PREP TIME
10 minutes

COOK TIME
40 minutes

BERRYLICIOUS CRUMBLE

FOR THE FILLING

3 cups fresh or frozen berries

2 tablespoons lemon juice

1 tablespoon arrowroot flour

½ teaspoon ground cinnamon

FOR THE CRUMBLE

¼ cup melted coconut oil

1 tablespoon maple syrup

1 cup rolled oats

½ cup almond meal

1 teaspoon ground cinnamon

Pinch of sea salt

TO SERVE

Dollop on some of your favourite yoghurt.

This is a crowd pleaser you can prep in 10 minutes and bake while serving dinner. Not only is this dessert incredibly delicious, but it's also packed with nutrition. The berries are rich in immune-boosting antioxidants and vitamin C, while the crumble has a great fibre content that promotes good digestion. You'll be surprised how simple the ingredients are for how incredible it looks (and smells!) when it comes out.

Preheat the oven to 180°C (360°F).

In an ovenproof dish, mix the filling ingredients together until the berries are well coated.

For the crumble, mix the coconut oil and maple syrup together. Then add the remaining crumble ingredients and stir until well combined.

Pour the crumble evenly over the berry mixture and bake in the oven for 30–40 minutes or until golden.

SWAPSIES

You can use any berries you like and both fresh or frozen work well.

The berry filling can also be swapped for most other fruits: stewed rhubarb and pear is one of our faves.

Arrowroot or tapioca flour is our go-to to mix through with the berries. However any flour will work as a substitute.

STORAGE

Store in the fridge for up to 2 days. You can also store the dish uncooked in the freezer for up to 3 months. When ready to serve, thaw and bake in the oven as per the method.

SERVES
Will depend on your ice block mould

PREP TIME
2 minutes

COOL TIME
4 hours

AGE
6 months +

MANGO ICE BLOCKS

Two-ingredient ice blocks? Yes please! We guarantee these refreshing and nutritious ice blocks will keep your little one happy for at least three and a half minutes! In fact, they're a warm-weather fave for the whole family.

1 cup frozen mango
¼ cup coconut milk/cream

Add the ingredients to a blender and blitz until smooth.

Pour into your mould of choice.

Freeze for at least 4 hours, pop them out and enjoy!

STORAGE

Store in the ice block moulds in the freezer for up to 2 months.

JELLY-TIP ICE BLOCKS

¼ cup Berry good jam (page 275)
1 cup yoghurt of choice

Add 2 teaspoons of jam to each ice block mould followed by 2 tablespoons of yoghurt.

Freeze for at least 4 hours, pop them out and enjoy!

STORAGE

Store in the ice block moulds in the freezer for up to 2 months.

AGE
18 months +

SERVES
4

PREP TIME
5 minutes

COOL TIME
3 hours

BERRY RIPPLE ICE CREAM

This banana ice cream with a berry ripple is a simple yet sensational dessert that requires only one ingredient for the base: frozen bananas! It is a healthy, nutritious and incredibly delicious ice cream that the whole family will love.

6 peeled frozen bananas
2 tablespoons Berry good jam (page 275)

Blend the frozen bananas until smooth.

Pour into a lined baking tin, mix through the Berry good jam and leave to set in the freezer for 3 hours.

STORAGE

Store in the freezer for up to 1 month in an airtight container.

TO SERVE

Finish it off with a drizzle of Choc magic shell (page 298).

CHOC MAGIC SHELL

Get ready to bring back the nostalgic childhood memories with this choc magic shell topping. Made with simple pantry ingredients, our take is quick and easy and sets on any frozen treat. We love getting our little ones involved in making this chocolate sauce, and they love cracking into it even more! Drizzle it generously over your favourite frozen treats and even add some extra toppings like puffed quinoa or finely chopped nuts.

¼ cup coconut oil
¼ cup raw cacao powder
2 tablespoons maple syrup

TOPPINGS
Puffed quinoa
Crumbled freeze-dried berries
Finely chopped nuts

Melt the coconut oil in a small saucepan.

Use a hand whisk to whisk in the cacao powder and maple syrup.

Pour it over our Berry ripple ice cream and watch it set like magic!

STORAGE

Enjoy this chocolate straight out of the fridge or freezer as it melts as quickly as it sets!

SERVES
72 drops

PREP TIME
10 minutes

COOL TIME
3 hours

AGE
6 months +

FROYO MELTS

These are tiny, cold, tasty bursts of flavour! They are a great go-to for relieving your little one's teething woes or as a fun addition to any meal. Also perfect for a moment of peace when they are tugging at your leg waiting for dinner to be ready. Your little one will be gobbling these up quicker than they can melt!

1 cup yoghurt of choice
½ cup mixed berries (or fruit of choice)
1 tablespoon LSA (optional)

Blitz all the ingredients in a blender until smooth.

Place teaspoons of the mixture on a baking tray lined with baking paper, or a silicone mat with a freezer-safe board underneath. Freeze for 3 hours.

Once the liquid has set, peel them off the baking paper and store in a jar in the freezer.

SWAPSIES

Swap LSA for ground linseed (flax seed) or leave out.
Spinach and mango are also fun variations to these melts.

STORAGE

Store in the freezer in an airtight container.

AGE
6 months +

SERVES
Makes 4–6 pops

PREP TIME
5 minutes

COOL TIME
4 hours

SMOOTHIE POPS

SMOOTHIE OF CHOICE:

Chocolate thickshake (page 163)

Superhero smoothie (page 164)

Berry blast smoothie (page 167)

Beat the heat with one of our favourite hacks for using up leftover smoothies. They're great for hot days, relieving sore gums or getting a boost of vitamins, minerals and antioxidants into your mini food critics.

Blitz all of your smoothie ingredients in a blender until smooth and creamy.

Pour into your ice-block moulds of choice.

Freeze for at least 4 hours, pop them out of the moulds and enjoy!

STORAGE

Store in the freezer for up to 3 months.

SERVES
12 small bars

PREP TIME
10 minutes

COOL TIME
3 hours

AGE
12 months +

BUBBLE BARS

Our twist on a rice bubble bar features puffed quinoa and has generous doses of fibre, healthy fats, protein and omega-3s.

- 1½ cups puffed quinoa
- ¼ cup LSA
- ¼ cup smooth peanut butter (or nut butter of choice)
- ⅓ cup Date paste (page 268)

In a large mixing bowl, add the puffed quinoa and LSA and stir to combine. Add your nut butter and date paste and mix well.

Pour the mixture into a freezer-safe tray and press down firmly. Place in the freezer to set for 3 hours.

Cut lengthways into six bars and again into halves for twelve smaller bite-sized pieces.

SWAPSIES

Puffed quinoa can be swapped for rice puffs or crumbled rice cakes.

STORAGE

Best stored in the freezer in an airtight container for up to 3 months.

AGE
12 months +

SERVES
Makes 1 large loaf or 8 slices

PREP TIME
10 minutes

COOK TIME
30 minutes

SUNSHINE LOAF

3 large eggs (or 4 small eggs)
⅓ cup extra-virgin olive oil
¼ cup honey*
1 teaspoon vanilla extract
1 tablespoon lemon juice
zest of 1 lemon
2 cups almond meal
1 teaspoon baking powder
½ teaspoon bicarbonate of soda (baking soda)

**Omit honey for babies under 12 months.*

This zesty lemon 'sunshine' loaf is packed with protein and healthy fats, and is deliciously light and fluffy thanks to the richness of the eggs and almonds. It's very yummy served with butter or nut butter as an afternoon snack or as a dessert the whole family will love.

Preheat the oven to 180°C (360°F). Line a loaf (bar) tin with baking paper.

Mix all the wet ingredients together in a large mixing bowl.

Stir through the dry ingredients until the mixture is well combined.

Pour the mixture into the loaf loaf tin and bake for 30 minutes. The loaf is ready when a knife inserted in the middle comes out clean.

Leave the loaf for 10 minutes to cool before removing from the tin. Transfer to a wire rack and let cool completely.

STORAGE

Store in the fridge for up to 6 days in an airtight container or in the freezer for up to 3 months.

SERVES
4

PREP TIME
5 minutes

AGE
24 months +

CHOCCY MOUSSE

This beautiful nutrient-dense dessert only takes 5 minutes to whip up. This dish is full of antioxidants from the cacao and nourishing fats from the avocado. This silky-smooth nourishing dessert will have you dreaming about avocado season all year round.

¼ cup maple syrup
2 ripe avocado, flesh scooped out
3 tablespoons raw cacao powder
1 teaspoon vanilla extract
½ cup coconut cream

Blitz all the ingredients in a blender until smooth and well combined.

SWAPSIES

Swap coconut cream for coconut milk or milk of choice.

STORAGE

Store in the fridge in an airtight container and eat within 1 day (if it lasts that long!).

INDEX

A

additives 82
allergens, food 40
  frequency 44
  introducing 42
  master guide 46–9
allergic reaction 45
  treatment 45
almond
  Bable birthday cake 293
  Chewy cookies 289
  Festive cookies 290
  Nana zuke bread 135
  Nutty cookie dough balls 144
  Sunshine loaf 306
  Thumbprint muffins 159
apple
  Bable bircher 98
  Bouncy brekky bites 101
Apricot delights 147
avocado
  Beanie nachos 238
  Chips 'n' guac 255
  Choccy mousse 309
  Superhero smoothie 164

B

Bable baked beans 106
Bable bircher 98
Bable birthday cake 293
Bable cereal 118
Bable crumb 264
baby cereal 32
baby food pouches 33
Baby-led weaning 20–1
  fun with finger foods 22–3
  pros and cons 21
bananas
  Berry good banana bread 143
  Berry ripple ice cream 298
  Chocolate thickshake 163
  Custard oats 102
  Easy-freezey pancakes 122
  Easy-peasy cookies 152
  Nana zuke bread 135
  Superhero smoothie 164
  Thumbprint muffins 159
  Turbo muffins 140
Beanie brownie bites 282
Beanie nachos 238
beans, Bable baked 106
beef
  Burger and chippies 241
  Meatballs and veggie sauce 234
  Mighty veggie bolognese 218
  No-pasta lasagne 217
beetroot
  Crispy rainbow chippies 252
  Heartbeet pancakes 97
  Pink hummus 272
  Red velvet balls 139
Berry blast smoothie 167
Berry good banana bread 143
Berry good jam 275
Berrylicious crumble 294
Berry ripple ice cream 298
Berry yummy gummies 148
besan (chickpea flour)
  Berry-good banana bread 143
  Chickpea pancrêpes 114
  Easy-peasy crêpes 150
bircher, Bable 98
Blondie bites 285
blood sugar 68
blueberries
  Bable cereal 118
  Berry blast smoothie 167
  Berry good jam 275
  Berrylicious crumble 294
  Bouncy brekky bites 101
  Broth blocks 175
  Chickpea pancrêpes 114
  Easy-freezey pancakes 122
  Everything oats 113
  Fluffy custard sticks 109
  Thumbprint muffins 159
bone broth
  Bouncy brekky bites 101
  Broth blocks 175
  Chicken soup 213
  Everything oats 113
  Hearty lentil soup 225
  Quinoa wraps 263
Bouncy brekky bites 101
  Fluffy custard sticks 109
bread
  Berry good banana bread 143
  Burger and chippies 241
  Chicken schnitty 214
  Chips 'n' guac 255
  Fluffy custard sticks 109
  Nana zuke bread 135
  Oat wraps 259
  Pizza 242
  Quesadillas 199
  Quinoa wraps 263
  Yoghurt flatbreads 256
breastmilk 31
  Breastmilk, formula and other liquids 31
Brekky baked eggs 121
broccoli
  Cheesy broccoli bombs 200
  Creamy coconut fish curry 226
  Green frittata 230

Mean green pasta 221
Rainbow fish bake 245
Roast chook 206
Veggie lentil curry 233
Broth blocks 175
Bubble bars 305
Burger and chippies 241
butter, Seed 267

C

cacao
Beanie brownie bites 282
Chia pudding – three ways 117
Choccy-baked oats 125
Choccy crackles 286
Choccy mousse 309
Choccy spread 276
Chocolate thickshake 163
Zesty lamington balls 136
cake, Bable birthday 293
caged 80
calcium 57
carrots
Bable birthday cake 293
Sweet 'n' sticky carrots 260
capsicum
Bable baked beans 106
Little veggie sausage rolls 203
Secret sauce 209
carbohydrates 68
cauliflower
Chocolate thickshake 163
Mac 'n' cheese 196
Secret sauce 209
Veggie lentil curry 233
Veggie-packed shepherd's pie 246
cheese
Bable birthday cake 293
Beanie nachos 238
Cheesy broccoli bombs 200
Cheesy fritz 126
Egg poppers 171
Mac 'n' cheese 196
Mighty veggie muffins 168
No-pasta lasagne 217
Pizza 242
Zesty pesto 271
Chewy cookies 289
chia seeds
Apricot delights 147
Berry good jam 275
Berry yummy gummies 148
Chia pudding – three ways 117
Crunchy seed snaps 155
Nutty cookie dough balls 144
Zesty lamington balls 136
chicken
Chicken schnitty 214
Chicken soup 213
Hug-in-a-cup broth 279
Roast chook 206
Zesty pesto pasta 210
Chickpea pancrêpes 114
chickpeas
Blondie bites 285
Creamy coconut fish curry 226
Falafel bites 192
Gooey chickpea cookies 151
Pink hummus 272
Three-ingredient power balls 132
chocolate
Beanie brownie bites 282
Blondie bites 285
Choccy-baked oats 125
Choccy crackles 286
Choccy spread 276
Choc magic shell 132, 298
Chocolate thickshake 163
Festive cookies 290
Gooey chickpea cookies 151
Three-ingredient power balls 132
chippies, Burger and 241
Chips 'n' guac 255
Choccy-baked oats 125
Choccy crackles 286
Choccy spread 276
Choc magic shell 132, 298
choking 26
choline 61
citrus fruits 49
coconut
Apricot delights 147
Beanie brownie bites 282
Creamy coconut fish curry 226
Creamy mango squishies 160
Munchy muesli bites 156
Red velvet balls 139
Veggie lentil curry 233
Zesty lamington balls 136
Combo-feeding 24
pros and cons 24
cookies
Chewy cookies 289
Gooey chickpea cookies 151
Easy-peasy cookies 152
Festive cookies 290
cow's milk 31, 50
swaps 50
Creamy coconut fish curry 226
Creamy mango squishies 160
crêpes
Chickpea pancrêpes 114
Easy-peasy crêpes 150
Crispy rainbow chippies 252
crumble, Berrylicious 294
Crunchy seeds snaps 155
curry
Creamy coconut fish curry 226
Veggie lentil curry 233
custard
Custard oats 102
Fluffy custard sticks 109

D

dairy 80
dates
Apricot delights 147
Bubble bars 305
Chewy cookies 289
Choccy mousse 309
Date paste 268
Gooey chickpea cookies 151
Munchy muesli bars 156
Nutty cookie dough balls 144

Red velvet balls 139
Three-ingredient power balls 132
Zesty lamington balls 136

E

Easy-freezey pancakes 122
Easy-peasy cookies 152
Easy-peasy crêpes 150
egg 50
Brekky baked eggs 121
Chickpea pancrêpes 114
Egg poppers 171
Green eggs, no ham 129
Green frittata 230
Quinoa rainbow rice 229
replacements 50
Speedy spinach omelette 110
Everything oats 113

F

Falafel bites 192
farming practices 80
fats 70
Festive cookies 290
fibre 73
fish 51, 81
Creamy coconut fish curry 226
Rainbow fish bake 245
Salmon bites 188
Super sardine bites 191
The Med pasta 222
flaxseed
Bable crumb 264
Red velvet balls 139
Crunchy seeds snaps 155
Zesty lamington balls 136
flatbreads, Yoghurt 256
Fluffy custard sticks 109
formula 31
Breastmilk, formula and other liquids 31
food quality 74
free-range 80
frittata, Green 230
fritter
Cheesy fritz 126
Froyo melts 301
fruit 69
fullness cues 30

G

Gagging vs. choking 26
checklist 27
gelatin
Berry yummy gummies 148
Bouncy brekky bites 101
Creamy mango squishies 160
Supercharged squishies 172
gluten 48, 51
GMOS 80
Gooey chickpea cookies 151
Green frittata 230
grain-fed produce 80
grass-fed meat and poultry 80
Green eggs, no ham 129
gut health 73

H

Heartbeet pancakes 97
Hearty lentil soup 225
heavy metals 74
hemp seeds
Bable crumb 264
Speedy spinach omelette 110
Super sardine bites 191
honey 48
Hug-in-a-cup broth 279

I

ice blocks
Jelly-tip ice blocks 297
Mango ice blocks 297
ice cream, Berry ripple 298
iodine 58
iron 54
haem sources 54
high-iron recipes 55
non-haem sources 54

J

jam, Berry good 275

L

lamb, Slow-cooked 237
lasagne, No-pasta 217
legumes 79
Bable baked beans 106
Beanie nachos 238
Hearty lentil soup 225
Little veggie sausage rolls 203
soaking 79
Veggie lentil curry 233
Veggie-packed shepherd's pie 246
Little veggie sausage rolls 203
LSA (linseeds, sunflower seeds, almonds)
Bable crumb 264
Bubble bars 305
Froyo melts 301

M

Mac 'n' cheese 196
magnesium 59
mango
Chia pudding – three ways 117
Creamy mango squishies 160
Mango ice blocks 297
Mean green pasta 221
Meatballs and veggie sauce 234
Mighty veggie bolognese 218
Mighty veggie muffins 168
milk, cow's 31, 50
swaps 50
Monster pancakes 94
muesli bars, Munchy 156
muffins
Mighty veggie muffins 168
Turbo muffins 140
Munchy muesli bars 156

N

nachos, Beanie 238
Nana zuke bread 135
No-pasta lasagne 217
nutrition labels 82
nut butter 51, 59, 89
nuts
  Bable birthday cake 293
  Bable cereal 118
  Berry blast smoothie 167
  Blondie bites 285
  Bubble bars 305
  Chewy cookies 289
  Chia pudding – three ways 117
  Choccy-baked oats 125
  Choccy spread 276
  Chocolate thickshake 163
  Easy-peasy cookies 152
  Gooey chickpea cookies 151
  Nana zuke bread 135
  Nutty cookie dough balls 144
  Sunshine loaf. 306
  Superhero smoothie 164
  Thumbprint muffins 159
Nutty cookie dough balls 144

O

oats
  Bable bircher 98
  Bable cereal 118
  Berrylicious crumble 294
  Bouncy brekky bites 101
  Chewy cookies 289
  Choccy-baked oats 125
  Easy-freezey pancakes 122
  Easy-peasy cookies 152
  Everything oats 113
  Heartbeet pancakes 97
  Munchy muesli bars 156
  Nutty cookie dough balls 144
  Oat wraps 259
  Red velvet balls 139
  Turbo muffins 140
oils and fats for cooking 71
omega-3 fatty acids/ DHA 60
omelette, Speedy spinach 110
orange
  Supercharged squishies 172
  Zesty lamington balls 136
organic 80
  buying 77
other liquids, Breastmilk, formula and 31

P

pancake
  Chickpea pancrêpes 114
  Easy-freezey pancakes 122
  Heartbeet pancakes 97
  Monster pancakes 94
pantry staples 89
pasta
  Mac 'n' cheese 196
  Mean green pasta 221
  Meatballs and veggie sauce 234
  Mighty veggie bolognese 218
  The Med pasta 222
  Zesty pesto pasta 210
paste, Date 268
pastry
  Little veggie sausage rolls 203
pasture-raised meat and poultry 80
peanuts 51
  Berry blast smoothie 167
  Blondie bites 285
  Bubble bars 305
  Choccy-baked oats 125
  Chocolate thickshake 163
  Easy-peasy cookies 152
  Gooey chickpea cookies 151
  Nana zuke bread 135
  Nutty cookie dough balls 144
peas
  Cheesy broccoli bombs 200
  Cheesy fritz 126
  Creamy coconut fish curry 226
  Egg poppers 171
  Falafel bites 192
  Green eggs, no ham 129
  Green frittata 230
  Mean green pasta 221
  Mighty veggie muffins 168
  Quinoa rainbow rice 229
pepitas
  Bable cereal 118
  Crunchy seeds snaps 155
  Munchy muesli bars 156
  Seed butter 267
pesticides 76
pesto, Zesty 271
pie, Veggie-packed shepherd's 246
Pink hummus 272
Pizza 242
plant-based milks 80
pops, Smoothie 302
pouches, baby food 32
poultry 80
  pasture-raised 80
prebiotics 72
probiotics 72
protein 69
pudding – three ways, Chia 117
Purée combos 18–9

Q

Quesadillas 199
quinoa
  Bable cereal 118
  Bubble bars 305
  Cheesy broccoli bombs 200
  Quinoa rainbow rice 229
  Salmon bites 188
  Super sardine bites 191
  Quinoa wraps 263

R

Rainbow fish bake 245
raspberry
  Berry-good banana bread 143
  Berry good jam 275
  Berrylicious crumble 294
  Berry ripple ice cream 298
  Berry yummy gummies 148

Broth blocks 175
Froyo melts 301
Jelly-tip ice blocks 297
Turbo muffins 140
Red velvet balls 139
rice
Bable rice 118
Choccy crackles 286
Quinoa rainbow rice 229
Sushi 195
Roast chook 206

S

Salmon bites 188
sardine bites, Super 191
sauce, Secret 209
sausage rolls, Little veggie 203
Seed butter 267
schnitty, Chicken 214
seasoning 36
Secret sauce 209
sesame seeds
Crunchy seeds snaps 155
Quinoa rainbow rice 229
Slow-cooked lamb 237
smoothies
Berry blast smoothie 167
Chocolate thickshake 163
Smoothie pops 302
Superhero smoothie 164
soaking legumes 79
sodium 34
swaps 34
soup
Chicken soup 213
Hearty lentil soup 225
soy 51
swaps 51
Speedy spinach omelette 110
spinach
Easy-peasy crêpes 150
Monster pancakes 94
Smoothie pops 302
Speedy spinach omelette 110
Superhero smoothie 164
spoon-feeding 17
pros and cons 17
starting solids 8
equipment 13
how much and how often 28–9
first tastes 10
fullness cues 30
readiness signs 9, 10
sugar 36
sunflower seeds
Bable cereal 118
Crunchy seeds snaps 155
Munchy muesli bars 156
Seed butter 267
Zesty pesto 271
Sunshine loaf 306
Supercharged squishies 172
Superhero smoothie 164
Super sardine bites 191
Sushi 195
Sweet 'n' sticky carrots 260
sweet potatoes
Beanie nachos 238
Burger and chippies 241
Crispy rainbow chippies 252
Hearty lentil soup 225
Mighty veggie muffins 168
No-pasta lasagne 217
Roast chook 206
Secret sauce 209
Veggie lentil curry 233

T

tahini
Bable cereal 118
Munchy muesli bite 156
Three-ingredient power balls 132
The Med pasta 222
Three-ingredient power balls 132
Thumbprint muffins 159
tomato
Brekky baked eggs 121
Egg poppers 171
Hearty lentil soup 225
Meatballs and veggie sauce 234
Mighty veggie bolognese 218
Rainbow fish bake 245
Secret sauce 209
The Med pasta 222
Veggie-packed shepherd's pie 246
toxic load 74
tree nuts 51
Turbo muffins 140

V

Veggie lentil curry 233
Veggie-packed shepherd's pie 246
vitamin A 62
vitamin B12 63
vitamin C 55, 64
vitamin D 65

W

wheat and gluten 51
wraps
Oat wraps 259
Quinoa wraps 263

Y

yoghurt
Froyo melts 301
Jelly-tip ice blocks 297
Yoghurt flatbreads 256

Z

Zesty lamington balls 136
Zesty pesto 271
Zesty pesto pasta 210
zinc 56
zucchini
Beanie nachos 238
Creamy coconut fish curry 226
Mac 'n' cheese 196
Mean green pasta 221
Mighty veggie muffins 168
No-pasta lasagne 217
Quinoa rainbow rice 229
Rainbow fish bake 245
Roast chook 206
Superhero smoothie 164

THANKS

To Frankie and George, our first babies. You two were our inspiration for starting Bable and ultimately to write this book and help other parents nourish their children the same way we love to nourish you. Thank you for trying our food and giving us your honest feedback (by spitting it out or gobbling it up!). Thank you for helping us to find our purpose and inspiring this wonderful brand that we hope will continue to make an impact and be a guide to so many families out there.

To our supportive husbands Andy and Kimon for giving us space and encouragement to create this book, and for never once doubting us on this journey and of course for taste-testing Every. Single. Recipe. (A special mention to Kimon for cleaning up after us at every photoshoot.)

To our Bable community and all the wonderful people who put their hand up to taste test our recipes for this book! We wouldn't be here without you engaging with us and following along so closely. We hope to continue to inspire you to offer your little ones nourishing choices.

To our wonderfully talented photographer Jess, it was excitement at first sight and we always knew you could deliver our vision. Thank you for bringing this book to life, it was such a pleasure working with you and your beautiful energy.

To our amazing publisher Alice and the wider Hardie Grant team, thank you for finding us and believing in this book as much as we do. To our project editor Tahlia who took us on as her first project back from maternity leave, thank you for making our meanders sound palatable.

And last, but *definitely* not least, thank you to all the readers! Thank you for supporting us and purchasing this book. We hope it makes your busy lives as parents feel a little easier, takes the guesswork out of making nourishing meals for you and your family and, at the very least, makes your tastebuds very happy. We are forever grateful.

ABOUT THE AUTHORS

LAUREN SKORA

Lauren holds a Bachelor of Design with Honours in Visual Communications and became a published author at 23 years old. She spent a decade working in the fashion industry, specialising in graphic design, marketing and creative direction.

Although her first love is design, she became passionate about baby nutrition after having her daughter, Frankie. She's since become a certified nutrition consultant, specialising in babies. Lauren melded her knowledge of design and nutrition to make Bable the go-to place for everyday food hacks and simple, highly nutritious recipes the whole family will enjoy.

JULIA TELLIDIS

Jules spent the first ten years of her career in the corporate world. After becoming increasingly frustrated by how people around her didn't take good care of themselves and their bodies, she jumped ship to start her studies in clinical nutrition.

Five years later, Jules now holds a certificate in health coaching, an Advanced Diploma of Nutritional Therapeutics and a Graduate Diploma of Human Nutrition. She is passionate about holistic health and Bable's 'food is medicine' philosophy. After she had her first child, George, she felt compelled to use her knowledge and learnings to educate other new parents. Jules' goal for Bable is to help all parents feel empowered about making better nutritional decisions in the crucial first years of their child's life.

Published in 2024 by Hardie Grant Books, an imprint of Hardie Grant Publishing

Hardie Grant Books (Melbourne)
Wurundjeri Country
Building 1, 658 Church Street
Richmond, Victoria 3121

Hardie Grant Books (London)
5th & 6th Floors
52–54 Southwark Street
London SE1 1UN

hardiegrant.com/books

Hardie Grant acknowledges the Traditional Owners of the Country on which we work, the Wurundjeri People of the Kulin Nation and the Gadigal People of the Eora Nation, and recognises their continuing connection to the land, waters and culture. We pay our respects to their Elders past and present.

A catalogue record for this book is available from the National Library of Australia

Baby Food Bible: A Nourishing Guide to Feeding Your Family, from First Bite and Beyond
ISBN: 9781761450303

10 9 8 7 6

Publisher: Alice Hardie-Grant/Tahlia Anderson
Design Manager: Kristin Thomas
Designer: George Saad
Design Coordinator: Celia Mance
Photographer: Jessica Belnick
Typesetter: Hannah Schubert
Head of Production: Todd Rechner

Colour reproduction by Splitting Image Colour Studio
Printed in China by Leo Paper Products LTD.

The paper this book is printed on is from FSC®-certified forests and other sources. FSC® promotes environmentally responsible, socially beneficial and economically viable management of the world's forests.